)O(

Crowned:

Becoming the Woman of my Dreams

The Missing Things were Goddess Wings

Poems, Prayers & Love Letters

By Sherry Sharp

~

Copyright © 2015 Sherry Sharp

All rights reserved.

ISBN: -10 1517740401
ISBN-13: 978-1517740405

I dedicate this book to my Husband Brent & Children: Kelsey, Hunter & Eric. You are my All. My Everything. My Joy. There is no life for me without you all by my side. I have explored so many sides of my womanhood in this lifetime. Still, my highest moments as a woman on this planet, are twofold. Wife. Mother. I would lay down my life for your every happiness. I love you with an eternal beating love that crosses time, space and back again.

Your support of my Goddess Journey has meant so much to me.

)O(

To my Goddess Mother, you came looking for me.
I was Dark inside.
And I stood out in the Dark, with the Moon & Stars, the wind and the rain, the snow and the ice, almost every night looking for something or someone to fill me.
I didn't know why I went out, I just knew I had to be there.
And the first time You spoke, I heard: You are done with this now.
Let in the Light.
You are so loved. You are so loved. You are so loved.
Let in the Light.
Your rose up in me, and I rose to my life.
For your faith in me, I will eternally find a way now to gather, heal and nurture women in your name.

This is my promise to you.

"Determined to save her own life, she wore only white. And in one year alone, wrote 366 poems."

~Marion Woodman

"I know a person who, though no poet, composed some verses in a very short time, which were full of feeling and admirably descriptive of her pain: they did not come from her understanding, but, in order the better to enjoy the bliss which came to her from such delectable pain, she complained of it to her God. She would have been so glad if she could have been cut to pieces, body and soul, to show what joy this pain caused her.

~Teresa of Ávila, The Life of Saint Teresa of Ávila by Herself

Prologue

I used to be a Wish.
Until I woke up, and became a Dream come true.

These words, like all the word-weaving in this book, just came to me. Just as if they were gifts to be opened. When they were ready to be born, I could not write them down fast enough. There were times I went back and read them, wondering who wrote them. Was it really me? Who was this new me, that saw things this way? Over the last few years of my emergence and awakening to the Divine Feminine, to the marvelous idea of God as Woman, to the idea of Goddess Within and through me; I have been tested. Though life came hard with loss at times, the words of these poems, prayers, musings and essays, came easy. What I see now is that they are from HER. To me. To you. They are the love from the loss. The Love Letters.

SHE has taught me all about the many forms of Love. All about hard-core self-love first, healing by giving , allowing my creative abandon, feeling my feelings, Nature as the greatest spiritual teacher, respect for this planet we are graced to live on, the gifts, lessons and power of my dark shadows, reaching for the light daily, seeing the magic, feeling the Oneness, and being of service to other women (especially in the areas I needed to heal the most, to give what I needed to receive) And rising. Just keep rising.

Every woman has a gift. I have been called by Her to start a woman's poetry/art circle at a Woman's Transition Home Shelter. I have been called to write my Heartsoul out and put it out there into the world.
These are two things I never thought I'd have the courage to try. I did, and so can you. If you are on this planet, you have a divine plan to live out. It is your duty to cease holding back now. We all need you. Every heart matters. Every voice is a story that can save another life. You have a message. You are a messenger. The farther you have fallen, the more you have to share. My prayer is that one word, one phrase; one poem here prompts you to live your message. The Goddess doesn't want to be worshipped. She wants to serve on Earth as you, through you. SHE comes to her

resilience, her passionate intentions, her defiance of convention, her brightness and glory, her bonfire of magical living, her giving and receiving, her full emotional expression, her seeing the beauty and romance, her deep service to creating peace and unity on this planet through you.

I look back on these writings and see all my crusty, bloody places where I still need/ed to grow. They are not listed here in any order. They are all over back and forth messy truth. It's not about pretty or perfect, just real, just raw, just evolving more each day. I see now, it is the losses that have gained me the most. As I compiled the poems, rereading them as a whole, I came to the realization that though they may appear to have been written with certain others in mind, I was truly talking to a piece of myself every time I said: Please don't abandon me. Please love me. That is hard to say, but if I tell my truth, perhaps you can see and tell yours. I have more questions then I'll ever have answers for. I realize now that it doesn't have to have a wrapped up answer with a bow on top, to have had a purpose. The purpose was: love yourself more. Just keep loving yourself through it.
Deserve your life. Your dreams. See your worth and magnitude to be and give love that only you are.

Still, I feel my power building. I feel the fire inside that is the legs-wide-open Poetess, Creatoress of my Universe. I am the portal, as are you. I'm teaching myself to be my own healer, sister, goddess, daughter, wild woman, muse, medicine woman, friend, soulmate, enchantress, wise woman, priestess, lover, and Mother.

I hope one day soon, you will teach yourself, that all you need is contained within you as well.

I love women.
I love you so much.
You have no idea how I see your light.
It blinds me with faith for the future.

)o(

)O(

**All this time, how did I not see it.
The missing things were Goddess wings.**

Love Letter from the Goddess:

You are the Life giving blood of the Mother God.
She who birthed the Universe with every thrust of her hips.
Unhand the idea that God is only Man.
It is womb that held all of the Earth's creatures safe.
It is Her blood, Her amniotic fluid, Her milk that secures Life.
SHE is the one who will move mountains for her children.
It is She that will bloody her own hands tirelessly for those she loves.
Goddess Mother lives in you.
You have the Power to Rebirth yourself.
It will take time, the labor will be hard,
but you will hold the writhing newborn of you, if you so choose.
Reach into yourself now.
Deliver yourself.

The Poem of Me Begins

This was the year of looking deep into the caverns of my own eyes to see Goddess looking straight back at me. This is the year she said,

"Wake the hell up woman, there is hard and holy work to be done."

The year I finally said no to boomerangs, cannonballs, punching bags, shotguns, showdowns, playing hide and seek, hot and cold, and being put to the curb. The year I finally declared to me and them, I am worth the fight. I need a friend who is willing to hold me as I cry.

The year of reading and writing a thousand words of Surrender and gratitude. The year I ceased asking the same question a different way, and gave up all need for answers for someone else's actions.

This is the year I lowered myself naked, on my belly, fingers scraping rock, bruised and bleeding, but vehemently determined to tap my own wells for the muck, and the oil, and the fissures; for the betrayals and the diamonds of me.

For the lost treasure I became.

This is the year I got to the bottom of it, and I just sat there, silently thanking Goddess for every loss and abandonment and grief. I rubbed them all over my face, smelling them, tasting them, feeling them, hearing them, and I didn't even have to look up to the sky, because she was right there shining golden on my lips, and my fingertips.

This was the year I stopped playing the same old games. The year I chose conscious living and saw that choosing happiness is my only purpose and highest spiritual path.

This is the year I released the albatrosses, and called in the higher winged beings.

This is the year I sat at death's bed, and ushered the one I loved the most home, and somehow didn't burst and break into a million biting shard pieces. I took his tomb, and the tomb it gutted in me, and I made damn sure every week that I try to save a life with it. This year I realized that although I appear as soft flesh, and brittle bones, I have the red hot lava blood and the fucking home of Goddess right in my womb.

I am veined for transformation. Let the bloodletting begin.

This is the year I got called outside to be healed under the moon. This is the year I released impulses that did not serve me. The year I stared addiction in the face, mine and others. I saw clearly all the ways we project, deny, manipulate, rationalize, and lie to ourselves, all because we just want to be loved, and give love, and live love, and we are just so scared to claim it as deserved.

This was the year I finally fell in love with myself. The year I became my own soulmate and best friend. The year I looked in my eyes and said: I love you. I really love you.

This is the year I released their sins and mine. I allowed the humanness, I called in the Soul. The year I forgave. This is the year I released everything outside of it, and went into my sacred heart. This is the year I forgot to put on a mask.

I obeyed only HER voice.

This is the year I walked the woods, and prayed where I shit. I realized prayer is not always this pretty scripted process done in a pretty patterned dress in a pretty sunny place. Most of the time, it's done face down, in the dirty smelly muck of me. I don't want one way conversation, I want communion, union, and the tough mother love of Her.

This is the year I said, I'm a circle, I will not walk a line for anyone, certainly not for my frightened ego-self either. I am eternal, complete, ever renewing within and of myself.

This is the year I came to see, I Am the only map, song, book, church, guru, doctrine I need.

This is the year I got that true love shows up, allows your emotions, takes responsibility, and holds you when you think you might die of heartbreak, sees your strengths, has your back, listens to your soul, looks between the lines, and atones for hurting you. This is the year I drew boundary lines in the shifting sands. I stayed quiet and remembered what I deserve. Then I roared not from ego, but from The Seat of my Goddess Kali Soul.

I put on my beautiful crown. I became my own coronation.

This is the year I walked my talk. The year I gave back to everywoman I could, her own worth. The year I listened to a dragonfly tell me, "You were born to do this." The year the Goddess laid her temple inside my temple in the night. The year she asked, are you ready, you are about to undergo great transformation. The year I said, YES!

This is the year I just knew, what was over and what was beginning.

The year I stopped starving and beating on my body. The year I fed it soul food, and raging self-love. The year I called myself a Goddess Girl rising, so that other women could too. The year I replaced sleepless tiring obsessions, with becoming a White Witch conjuring her own magic.

The year I claimed I am only my Now. The year I said no one, but no one gets to drink my wine, and eat at my table and then label or judge me. The year I atoned, in my head, in my heart, in the shower, in my sleep, in the car, in the ocean, in bed. The year I said I'm sorry. I am truly sorry. The year I came back from the briars. The year I wrote: I am addicted to the woman I know I can become. I serve only that woman.

I search the hole of me for the whole of me. This was the year I became the woman of my dreams.

This is the year the poem of me truly began. The year I talked to trees and they talked back. The year I called in the Sister Love, communed with Nature and learned what it means to truly live as Witch. The year I evolved to calling myself a Priestess of The Goddess, serving her daughters. *The year I saw God as a woman.*

The year I took shelter at the Shelter, went into the woods with the lost girls, and came out found. The year I felt the Oneness of it all. I Am Her. She is me. We are Goddess incarnate. The year I became an Art Healer, Po-e-therapy Priestess, Queen of my kingdom, Earth angel seeking and serving the meek from my life-giving womb. I have shifted now. There is no going back.

This is the year I channeled my self-worth unabashedly. The year I declared: Fuck Humble! Screw hiding. *Everyone do something beautiful and kind and then tell the whole damn world about it!*

The year I said I'm going to Shine and give you permission to shine too. The year I "gypsied" on, knowing if the gypsy in me dies, I die. The year I saw women as the stars in the sky of Goddess that they truly are.

The year I claimed: I am a Light-worker. I am a rebel with an exalted cause. I see myself now. And I see you.

This is the year ambition just fell away, and I became moved only by inspiration. The year I finally told myself the truth about what abundance really is. The year I made videos and woman's circles, recited prayers, wrote prayers, meditated, journaled, felt the grass and the roots between my toes, the passion of the sun on my face, the winds of change, and the flames of my eternal gifts.

The year I called out, and they came in droves, into the light and dark of me. The year I met Brigit, Gaia, Mary Magdalene, Aphrodite, Luna, Kali, Coatlicue, Hecate, Demeter, Persephone, Eve, Pele, The Black Madonna, and finally saw mother Mary for who SHE is.

This is the year I drew her, and drew her in, until everything I never needed fell away, silently, knowingly, gently.

This is the year I realized loving from afar is not enough. The year I blessed it all, released it all, and finally chose me. The year I decided, I've split open, bleed out, and hand stitched myself back together. I've looked inside, I've awakened. Have your own awakening, and then we can talk, then I will listen, and I will listen with love's ears, but I can't save you from your way of thinking anymore.

This is the year sacred love became my new fixation. The year I escaped into myself. The year of solitude. Listening. The year I discovered the power of ritual, incantation, intuition, signs, energy, awareness, and intentions.

The year I realized the most powerful woman in the room is the one with the most love in her heart.

This was the year I loved my husband and children like the world was on fire and it was my last day here. The year I dreamed of dolphins, white light, the sea of love, the year I held my little inner girl child in my arms and told her it was really going to all be alright. The year of diamond eternity bands honed from coal, the year of my marriage to HER. The year I dreamed of forming circles, of women and candles, and truth.

The year Kundalini rose in my body, sang in my throat, and burned fierce from my third eye. The year I put snakes in their rightful place.

The year I felt Source's unconditional love swim with ecstasy inside me. The year I was told, you are loved beyond belief.

This is the year I learned the great truths of the Universe. Live out your passion. Serve others with it. It is your duty and work on Earth to do so. Speak your highest truth. I define me. Joy is my purpose. You get what you give. Search your Shadow, it's the only guru you need. Love yourself and then love yourself some more. And then more. And some more. Because Self-love is the answer to every question you ever had.

This year I knew, we are all one. We all matter. This year I heard: Call HER in. Let HER in. Embody HER. This year I named myself, Eternal flame Rising, Divine Feminine. This is the year I was summoned.
The year I was told, you will rise as hard as you fell. The year I was gifted with: you will teach many.

This is the year I stopped giving in, and began the journey of going in.

This is the year I asked all of myself, and I gave all of myself. This is the year of the Goddess. All of this in one year. I will never be the same. This is the year I was blessed, Beautiful One. All of this, and I am yet a Beginner.

A proud and ready Beginner.

Love Note from the Goddess:
)o(

You have been appointed. Your life awaits ruling.
Don the crown.

Prayer to the Triple Goddess
)o(

My Mother, My Goddess,
I kneel down to your powerful presence in my life,
The sands of time...
In thousands of crystal light particles at my feet.
I am every woman in one woman,
I am every stage,
And every age of Divine.
The sea of love, innately feminine,
In its ebbs and flows,
has my back~
Washes clean my toes.
I take my tender hands,
And form the beautiful, strong moons that are my birthright,
Half and full~
Waxing and waning~
As am I.

I place flower offerings,
In your bountiful center.
I light a flame to usher you into my soul.
Shells decorate your crescent curves,
You are beyond beautiful.
And the sea air whispers in my ear,
"As are you, my daughter dear" ~
A tear falls from my grateful eye,
For I know that nothing can ever wash you away from me now.

As you are All~
Wind, fire, sand and sea,
You are my altar.
I am your Maiden,
Young and free.
I am your Mother,
Nurturing and sensual.
I am your Crone,
Wise and Reborn.
I cry out your name~

Like the gulls crying overhead..

And I am in love,
And I am finally free.

Goddess Invocation
)o(

Moon mamma, Zen-goddess, praying a dance of illumination. I am she, she is me. Goddess washed away all my supposed sins, down by the everlasting sea.

Moon –Owned

She stood in the middle of the empty street,
Nothing on her feet,
Bare as the day she was born- (again)
Under the blood-letting moon,
Unafraid.
Sky serious and salmon-singed,
Holding tight to her tie-dyed dreams,
The last few years,
frantic fish swimming upstream.
She's really done now.
Tired of the sacrificing. Ready for the gleam.
You said you'd come, but you never came,
You said you'd stay, but you never stayed,
You said I love you…
But actions eat words for breakfast,
and lunch (and dinner).
Big to do,
To think something is forever.
Nothing that touches the dirt of this Earth is forever.

Just the sky with its clouds, its stars, its sun, its moon,
Like a witch, she paced her protective circles,
Offered it all up to the Mother,
Not a tear left to cry,
Or a single question of why.
It's been long enough now.
She tip-toed off to bed,
Imagery slipped (or maybe taken) from her head.
Peaceful pink of the eclipse
coming like a lover into her heart-body.
If you're lucky,
sometimes you end up right back where you started,
Blessed with Creator's care,
Held in original Divine plan,
With the destined-ones,
Alone, but never lonely,
and Moon-owned.

Goddess Worshipping
)o(
And the Mother said, you don't have to bow,
you have to Rise child.

(Tough) Love Letter from the Goddess:

I do not play. I will rip in and through you like a hurricane. I will burn you like a forest to the ground, to ashes, to be reborn. The wind will pick them up and send them where they truly need to be. I don't care about dogma, and ideology worship. My nudges may feel like bitch-slaps. That is because it's wake up time. I abhor idolization or promotion of me as only dainty and pure. My dress isn't always chiffon floating. It is flames roaring. I'm going to lick you up and down if you don't move towards yourself. Yes, my hair is wild and knotted. My gaze is crazed. I'm quite appalled that you won't see your glory. My love comes hot and seeking at you. For I am the end of the beginning for you. I expect you to do the work to slice out the cancers you no longer need in your life. Pick up your damn sword already! I want all of your darkness laid out like the Night Sky; let's see it I say, so we can understand its power over you. Screw being the most popular, pretty, successful, wealthy, loved, educated, intelligent, skinny, famous, desired woman in the room! I will bellow until you listen: what are your gifts! How are you using them to heal? To serve another? Forget looking outside you for answers. You are the answer and the question. Keep asking questions, until you get to the red, hot core of you. Answer every question with another question. Then let the lava flow until your soul burns, and lays upon all you touch. I am the apocalypse moving as you, through the world. It is not the world, but the way the world lives now, that must come to an end. Will you help me torch greed, competition, chains of command, abuse, starvation, disempowerment, famine, child prostitution, division, war, materialism, power-grubbing, ignorance, animal abuse, addictions, pollution of our environment and food, prejudice, human trafficking, religious terrorism, and inequality of any kind? It begins with each woman coming into her birthright divinity. Using herself as an entity of my fury. Will you smother this immensely beautiful power you own? I will only flame higher the next time. Until I consume you. Until My truth will burn you alive. Alive to who you are.

Hot and Holy

I lift my Spirit-pitcher high,
Firm grasp on my chosen Creator.
This moment, unadorned, unwitnessed.
So unlike the dirty river that flooded me here.
Freshly bathed with hot and holy water,
I sigh, inhale deep into the
kneeling of my seductive divinity,
I await no one...
I christen myself today,

With ancient waters,
Tears of the goddesses, long forgotten...
Born and buried no more.
Stone walls, fortresses once built high,
peel to reveal supple skin.
I face the light, so beautifully bright,
it kisses on my reverent, praying eyes,
Right down to the seat of my soul.
It's your dying day! Your birthday! Both today....
I will warrior forward,
Washed clean by your rapturous love,
But never covering my vulnerability.
The light caresses my breasts, my ribs,
Penetrates my heart...
I'm so beautiful in your light, I think,
I glow in the dark.

Love Note from the Goddess
)o(

Magic is your middle name. Circle round it now. Candlelit meditation is the way to call you up and out to your destiny.

Found in the Woods

I've never been one to follow a path for long,
Always felt a little lost, an acorn washed out to sea,
Wrong place, wrong time,
Drastic impossibility of ever becoming a tree.

I stood in the snow, at the edge of the woods,

At the edge of my life, and asked:
Show me the way Nature,
Endow me with SoulSight.
A cardinal red as a woman's blood shot right in front of me.
So there is hope for new life.

The woods, She is majestic incubation.
I tried not overwhelming her with all my concerns.

I walked and I listened,
And I spoke when I was spoken to.

I saw tracks, heard cracks from the columns of swaying trees,
Winter-hearty birds squawked at me,
Clumps of dried berries huddled together on bushes,
Tiny flakes fell delicate like angel tears on my frigid face...
Yet inside I was warmed,
Through and through,
By God's face all around, Goddess grace so true.

I sensed a broken tree, he called to me: please stop,
Completely cracked in half and over, he extended a plea,
I intuitively reached for his longest limb, stroked it lovingly.
I saw the broken in him; he saw the broken in me
I said I'm sorry you are hurt, but you are still loved, and yes,
You belong, you still belong.

I walked farther on, could have easily lost him,
but when I looped around,
He called to me again, said : I have something to say to you now.
You're on your way, it's going to be okay.
I breathed out, I breathed in,
Shook his little limb,
One more time.

Thank you.

I pitched my face to the sun, hid by gray clouds,

Winter's whitewashed way of streaming light,
And I thought, even when we can't see it or feel it,
It's nice to know it's always there,
It's so beautiful that it's always there.

I walked on.

Finally, stopping again to catch my breath,
I hugged a little tree, maybe ten inches round,
healthy as could be,
gazed down at a frozen stream below,
At the bank rising up across the way,
Took my one glove off to feel his healing bark,
Brought my heart right up to hug him.

A massive tree stood in the distance,
Now he has been here awhile,
must be wise I said to my new friend,

I sensed his urgency to be that tree...
Or was it just me,
Rushing ahead again.
And I reminded him that he lives in bliss,
No human frailties like the judgment of others to chop him down.

I made my way down
as close as I could come to the frozen stream,
Sensing its living flow under its ice,
Admired the tenacious dried leaves
clinging to the evergreen pines...

Life would resign, then go on...

I turned back, headed up the path again,
The little tree cajoled me to stay,
I said, I have to be on my way,
I'm human,
I'm not lucky enough to linger in the woods all day.

I'll come back to visit, I promised.
As I walked away, he told me his name
was Easter.

Easter? I smiled, on my way to the car...
Maybe Spring wasn't that far.

Today Winter gifted me SoulSight...
Seeing, giving and living from a place of deep-rooted renewal and
intense intuition.

I went in lost.
I came out found.

Goddess Portal
)o(

*All that is alive, wishes to come in, and out and through me.
I am the Door. The Passageway. The Bridge for life to be
born again, from the eclipse of fear to love.*

Inner Child Devotion
)o(

Dear Goddess Mother of Mine,
Let me carry my inner child upon my bosom,
upon my shoulders,
upon my neck,
wrapped safe where I can feel her.

Remind me she depends on me~
Wholly
to remind her she is Holy.
She has seen so much,
that a child should never see,
endured so much a child,
should not endure.

Still,
She can be complete fragility,
and complete brazen strength.
For she is a flesh and bones child of Goddess.
As I am there for her,
she is there for me.
Placing her gentle, small hand,
upon my crown,
She reminds me,
I may be little, but I am born of the Light, and
I live always just right of the glowing fight inside you.

Carry me, and I will carry you too.

You, Mother see my eternal perfection,
The strength in my fear,
and I declare now that you are Earth Priestess among women,
As you heal me,
You heal you.
As you heal you.
You heal others.

No one will ever love me,
like you do.

So love me, Mother~
Love me soft in all my hard places,
Lay me down each night, sacred,
Carry me each day into my holiness.

Goddess Renewal
)o(

I am a forest dwelling Gypsy Momma. Hanging with the trees of life. Exchanging breaths. This is my temple.

Goddess Invocation
)o(

Into the Cauldron

Sacred initiation of one,
Into oneness.
I grip the claw of The Dark Mother,
She has illuminated my Shadows.
I owe her my life.

Chin seared, body stark still, eyes fixed,
I dig my nails into what must be released.
I feel no pain.
I rest, at ease...naked, fearless
In the cauldron waters,
under the raging flames,
of the Great Mother.

Boiled alive, I die to live!
And come again as wind, water, fire, earth, spirit!
In the twilight hours, these are the titles I claim,
I Am...
Healer!
Gypsy!
Goddess!
Queen!

Witch!

I no longer fight destruction, as it is was my only True Love,
I no longer beg to make it real and right,
So I could say it was never wrong.
Demon lover, Haunted woman,
you scoured me clean into this fresh skin,
Grace sang out about all the things I never needed,
I finally came up to listen.

I live from Soul now.
Body be damned with her wanton needs,
Body be heralded for her secret sacredness.
I mold my body to Her pot only.
Smoke rises and clears from my mirrors,
The wine has been corked.
I am only Soul now.

I arch my back away from your deception,
Lips parted to blow self-betrayal away.
I take the Earth Mother deep into my mouth now,
Tasting her sweet nourishing flesh,
Roll around my tongue.

I have one job,
It is to love me.
Save me.
Heal me.

It's been a long time rising,
But I'm finally coming out of the cauldron.

Goddess Hide and Seek
)o(

And SHE said, "Let your Goddess out of the Closet."

I Started out a Hippie Child

My Inner Goddess
and my Inner Hippie Child...
have vacated the building.
They are running through the fields,
in flowing garments,
picking flowers,
singing like a choir of angels,
There on the riverbank...

they meet up with my Gypsy Poet Soul
They write a poem together,
about all the beautiful worlds,
they chose to see.
Along comes my Witch Healer,
She says; let's start a fire,
so large it can't be missed...
and they write all the sins
humans cast on each other down,
and burn them to a scorched nothingness in her cauldron.
My Goddess says: I co-created
this ancient planet, I still adore it,
though I have been relegated to the deep woods.
Man chose to tell man
that a man created all of life.
I have waited patiently to remind
the universe that the Feminine
is also necessary.
I bring you compassion, unity,
forgiveness, intuition, creativity,

emotion, beauty, unconditional love.
You will die without these.
They seem like tender things
But they are the most fierce and fearless of entities.
My Hippie Soul says: I will tell everyone; Love is all there is.
My Gypsy says, I will remind them to dance and explore.
My Witch Healer howls to the moon a prayer for Transformation.
and my Goddess rises up, hands extended to the Heavens.
She has birthed us.
Now we must birth her.
Every child has a Father and a MOTHER.

Goddess Beesechment
)o(

Dear Goddess,
I dream the same dreams in loops of obsession. They are dreams I'd like to sell. Dreams I have outgrown. Dreams that never bloomed. Or died young. As a picked flower, they had their glory day. Guide me toward gratitude for the gifts they were. Remind me that now that they are dead, I cannot watch them wither lifeless in the vase of my life forever. It is time to be vulnerable to fresh flowers pressed to the pages of my heart. I release the then. I embrace the now. So mote it be.

The Giving of the Night Souls

Crying black-night tears,
Goddess, where are you~
Come into my fallen angel-fears.

Are you strong enough to be fully vulnerable?
Only then will I come to you on a full moon's flowering,
Lay my essence into the mold of your willing body,
limb by limb~
Do you feel the divine perfect fit,
the unequaled bliss of me inside you?
There I sit, stretch...
and lay my healing.
Loud and clear, I hear
"How does it feel to have the Goddess dwell within you?"

Revealing herself the minute I asked her to,
The minute I did~

She powered through me, cracking my ribs open to get to my heart,
Within chaos, lies the start~

Blackbird, resting on the hip of the earth, start a flame in me...
Give me insight~
She squawks. Woman! You are cosmic magic...
Transcending time eternal,
Given-wings wasted ,are oil on fire at the feminine alter.
I will burn through you like the Earth's end,
If you squander your passions.

You beg of your purpose?
Seek-search, project it onto others,
in fleeting moments, in what you can hold in your hand...
Passions are purpose!
All sustenance has been laid at your feet with abandoned
abundance,
~Earth, air, water, fire~

Have you given gratitude to your Mother today?
Now, presently~
Poignantly inquire...
What have you returned to the Giver of Life?
Reciprocate!

The transformation of self, barrels in,
through the blood-letting , passionate ,sharing journey with another...
Birds fly together toward safe shelter,
Long distances, flocked, on goddess-breath,
Core-believe we are all one~
That what we take from this Earth-home we must replenish...

So much Love~
Breathtaking, unending love,
Given to you each breaking day...

Reciprocate with your soul...
You will never cry a night into morning again,
If you unfurl your soul's wings,
In service~
Your boiling passions,
Your raging talents,
Can save another fledgling...

There are only two things to be complete in this world~
Call your Goddess of Light in, then
Donate your soul
To another soul.

)o(

And Mother Moon whispers, "I am your Teacher now."

Sister Love Song
)o(

Goddess Mother, grant me the gift of true divine sisterhood.
The ones who pull their capes round them tight.
Cry at night.
Hand hold through the darkness.
Marry the light in each other.

The ones who do not pedestal or be jealous,
But love my messy bristled self.
That see and uphold my potential.
That call me kindly on my betrayals of self.
Remind me who I am and what my gifts are.
Let them love me fierce through the storms.
Have them send me back out when I am most afraid.
Allow my dalliances.
Praise my abundance.
The ones who talk deep.
Run hard into the woods.
Pray like birds in flight.
Allow the silences.
Burn judgments of me to the ground.
The ones who speak as if we are One Woman.

Let them come in droves, with flowers in their hair,
Dirt on their bare feet, sweat between their breasts,
tears in their eyes, looking for a kindred soul.
Let me lay my head in their lap and be all of me.
Let me bleed, cry, bellow, laugh, talk with them,
until the moon rises high in the night sky.

They won't leave me when the emotions flare.
That is when they pull me closer.
Let them honor my sensitivity and magic.

Come sisters! Come!

With your rituals, and poetry, your art, your song and dance.
Let us celebrate every day as our last and our first.
I've been waiting for you my whole life, she says to me.
I see you.
I know you.
I am you.

Let us grow like trees in the enchanted forest now.
Together, swaying in the wind's comfort.
Fire in our souls.
Wombs glowing hot golden light.
Grateful for the gift of truth in form.

Eye to Eye

Ours is a holy friendship
Angel-touched.
Honed as natural as stars,
To light the blackest sky.
Two worlds, oceans apart, yet eye to eye.
My net, my buoy, my knowing sigh.
And you said, "How long can you do this?"
How long can you be what you are not.
Until the day you die?
These are the crossroads.
The right words, at the right time, in the right tone.
So, I turned right. I became righteous. Righted. Path-driven.
Bearing home.

Goddess Free Fall
)o(

I have with care, walked the broken boardwalk,
to Discovering every nuanced sky-cloud of my soul.
Sometimes running too far ahead,
Sometimes lagging behind,
I ache to fly now.

I've rid myself of that scared, teased little girl,
That insecure young woman who compared herself to others,
That people pleasing woman that just wants everyone to love her.
I finally love my body.
See the brilliance of my heart.
The fire of my creativity.
The power of my intuition.
The strength of my thoughts to bring reality in line for me.
I act with attention and intention.
I finally understand that loving myself
is the greatest act of service,
I can shine on the universe...
For love begets love.

I have come to the end of this journey now,
I teeter on the edge of rebirth,

I believe it's time to free fall into all of me.

"Untuck your wings then..." You whisper.

"You were given them the day you were born...don't you see..
Now you know the secret...
Every
day
Is
Your
Birth Day.

The present is The Present.

What will you do with this sacred gift of your Present Soul?

Goddess Clarity Chant
)o(

*I Power Pose my way through life. Arms to her Sky. I am HER daughter. I survive. I thrive.
I rise again to every day. I am wild-hearted. I am open-souled. I Am an exalted tower.
I know my blessed Power.*

)o(

Prayer to She Who is Tree of Life

I see how you live in the trees,
Mother of leaf and bark,
Stream through them onto me.
I lift my face to your face.
For the light of you is the light of me.
I see how you love in the trees,
For they sway to your name,
Bend woodwind melodies for you.
I want to lay grounded in your dirt,
And die to you.
There is so much beauty in the quiet of me and you,
Alone in the woodsy-ways of energy exchange.
I breathe you in.

You breathe me out.
For a moment I am as tall as the trees that Goddess built.
Lost in the oneness.
Found in the green.
I am not a story of concrete, wheels, and microchips.
I am not the rush or ambition of more.
I am the legend of Avalon.
The daughter of magic.
The ecstasy of romance.
I am present to being in the beauty of the moment.
I am naturally myself.
I am protected by that which was here before me.
I am safely tucked in by the ferns and the flowers and seeds.
Lulled by the stream's flow.
Every sense is caressed to what feels like the home I've always searched for.
If the sun is this magnificent upon you, dare I think how the moon would fill and bewitch you and me?
I see how you seduce the truth out,
And it raises desire in me unspeakable,
To want to lie in your bed forever.
A forest-dweller devoted and vibrating to your call.

Goddess called: SHE left a message: BE Fearless!
)o(

I'm starting to really dissect the word Fearless. It's more than being Strong. We are all called to be strong many times over, but Fearless has a spiritual connotation to it. It suggests walking through the fire with Goddess at your side, knowing you are powerfully protected and guided. It's having the wisdom to call on Spirit in your life. It's having the inner eyesight to see the signs Spirit gives you every day. It's having the vulnerability and strength to take action you may be terrified of, but *know* you must do in order to save your soul.
Fearless.

I am Fearless
I walk away from that which no longer gives what it takes
I walk into the dark night alone
I walk into my soul's dark night
I walk into my soul
I walk out into the light

Offerings

I lit a silver tapered candle for Goddess today, then left the house
and walked as Essence.
Under the full moon. In cold circles warmed -through.
The wind bent the trees in yoga moves,
I heard them cry out: push me further, I have so much give.
What is my gift, I sing-songed lightly from my lips.
You are living it, SHE said. You stride with Joy.

You are a walking Dreamcatcher,
allowing the wind to blow the fear through,
and huddle the love in.
You are becoming a Queen of the Black sheep.
You took your shadow and made it dance for the better.
You said I'm done with not being full.
Full is an incantation I write daily now.

They said thanks for opening me to myself. I've waited so long for
this moment.
It is just you seeing you in me.
I give you back to yourself.
It's simple but no small thing to show someone the blessed in their
own soul.
Why don't we do it more often I wondered?
We are one woman walking the labyrinth.

And my moon blood came in a midnight gush of assurance.
So did my sister's.
A sign that we sculpt sisterhood,

where any harsh betrayal of self is cradled,
with sacred love that never says die.
We see each other.
I love her so.
We are crystals under the moon charging,
And healing.

This is the year of Mothering myself and them back.
A year of deep prayer towards true communion.

I see moons everywhere.
In the shower steam, by the light of my stained glass lamp.
I draw them on my hand, on my forehead,
like an everyday mystic.
I want to create sacred art and wipe another's tears.
I have wings I know the angels can show me how to use.
Her voice is a flame that flickers in me, tickling me out.

I went down to the creek, stood right where the bend of HER is,
I prayed, show me my path,
however it undulates,
I promise I will honor it.
I took a tumbled blue stone I brought as an offering,
And heaved it into Her Ever-flowing lap.
She swallowed it whole-heartedly,
and just like that it was One with Her.
Oh! How I wish I were that stone.

Goddess Magic
)o(

All that had eluded her, solitary dances, moonlit prances, wicked, prideful self-love. It came forceful into her now. Stood her on her toes. Ripped her heart wide open. Balanced her for the first time in her life. Centered her. Circled her. Illuminated her. I am every memory, every promise, every Now moment.

Glory is my life. Glory is what I claim for me. I am night. Moon-owned. Black as ink spilled across the trees. Wide-eyed as creatures that call my name. Wind-wet, whipping the breeze. I am starless. Stillness. I hang on every branch. Tease the leaves to flight. ~Glory. I am night

We are Wild Women Born of the Moon

There is that quote about how if one woman would just tell her truth, her darkness, her desires… the world would crack open.
One woman who says:
Here I go, straight into the black hole of me.
Into the new moon of all I can be.
I am a Ghost-Woman revisited, a Shadow-rider,
A wild-eyed, dirty-watered demon drinker.
Freezing me in a timeless, searching tizzy, (love's what's in front of you)
The rain pelts hard my dilated pupils,
One day, I'm going to run so far, no one will find me,
In my heart, it screws a good twist.
I need a year to find where I live.
Every gypsy needs a tramp into her soul.
There are days I want more or different or solitude or insanity.
I can't explain all of me, but I honor it anyway.

One woman, who tells her truth, frees another.
One woman who says: there are sides to me you don't even know.

I'm not crazy then, says the other woman…

I can be sweet and acidic.
I can be a homebody and a travelling nomad.
I can be a mother and an open-legged beast.
I can fold laundry and table dance in my head.
I can get lost in a book that feeds me or a man that drains me.
I can burn you and I can heal you.

I can drive to the brink and then turn around, or fall off the edge forever.
I can moisten every dryness of you.
I can hold your head in my lap and to my breasts.
I can have a corner of me that is lost to ever wanting to be found.
I can fly and I can burrow.
I can be wine-soaked and moon-lost for days on end.
Then I shop for toilet paper and life goes on.
I can shit where I pray and know its ok.
I can finally choose the peace of me too.
SHE loves me anyway. Any way. Every day. Every way.
I can write a poem to myself that says:
You don't get to judge me.
You created this that I am.
So you must want to see it all in action.
Here I am.
Every frayed fringe of me I offer up.
So that you can say:
I see you.
I see your truth.
I am your truth.
Thank you for the dirt and grub and missing parts of you exposed.
It's all part of the feminine jungle to have an underbelly.
It was man that bleached us untrue.

We are Wild Women.
Howlers. Blood-letters. Writhers. Magicians. Witches. Dirt-rollers.
Clawed. Open-fisted and hearted.
Ready to roll.

Goddess Proclamation
)o(

The freeze does not kill me. Underneath, I am Goddess blood beating. I know My fruit births the world. I am Priestess-Giver. Resilient healing Healer. Plump, and crimson hearted. I live to thaw the cynical souls into union with the sacredness. I am an everyday mystic sharing magic I've been gifted. Gracefully unfolding. Here is the secret knowledge you awaited all your life *So are you.*

I Manifest Easily

There comes a point, wise-one,
You swim out to the deepest part of the blue-black sea,
Paint your nails red,
Drown in yourself, who you used to be...
Moon shining down, tears pregnant on your face,
Think to yourself, it's such a
Disgrace
To come home every night
And detest me, all because you detest you.

A candle glowed Goddess-light under a wand of protection,
Roses died a slow death, sad in the shadows,
But the baby's breath lived on...

They are tenacious..
So am I.

Sigh.

I vow to write every day,
Every way a word can become whole..
I wish to be.

You said, you don't want me here,
And I said: no, not like this.
And the water was amiss,
And my life, once grounded,
Splashed salt into my eyes...
Burning my vision.

But She says, the way to pay the toll,
Is to go out and gather the others.

Swim back to shore, bring them out to their calling...
The abyss is destiny, marriage, salvation.

She birthed me,
Again .
Swallowed me whole.
Spit me out into the ocean,
Like the commotion I was.
Confetti sired on fire~

I emerged, a flock of sea-birds bursting from my chest,
I was called out.
I was called in.
A woman's circle tattooed in my heart.

Why do you have all these candles lit?
Well that's easy...
Because I need the light.
I crave the light.
I am the light.

And the light leads.

Love Letter from the Goddess
)O(
If you're hiding. You are stealing. You are betraying. You are lying. Do you understand my child? You are not living. If you are lying. You are dying.

Prayer to the Goddess
)O(

She-Wolf

Dear Mother,
Let me be like the wolf,
solitary in my staunch commitment
to self-survival.
Drawn by your moon-eye watching over me,
I shall hunt for my true self,
as a wolf hunts for her nourishment.

I am wolf-maiden howling a cry to the sky for birth.
Then I am life-giving Mother of the cubs of the Earth.
Finally, Ancient Wise Woman, Soul-teacher.
I run with knowing veracity,
through all phases of my Moon-being,
always seeking the ravaging She-wolf within,
the woman who shall never lie down and say die.
The woman devouring each beauty of the world she has been
given.

I hunt (seek) so that I may see and know
your majestic, benevolent presence.
For legend says you run wild in my veins,
burrow in my marrow,
knaw at my heart.
All these years, I felt, but didn't know who you were.

Inside you bellowed:

Let me pin you heavy to the ground.
Root you.
Sink my teeth into your fleshy brow.
The blood-letting shall release your noble Priestess,
Your sublime Light.
Trust.
Surrender.

My energy will surge through you until you cry for more!

The years I sought outside you, are lost lands to me now.
I have found you in the dark night,
in the dark night of my soul.

Release me under a Full Moon's night,
I am your daughter.
You are my Destiny.

Goddess Proclamation
)o(

Like the moon, like a rose, I am in full bloom, when I am under the spell of Self-Love.

Risen Woman

Throw your dirt.
Smear my face in it.
Lower the blow.
You didn't get all of me.
Expose more of your vision of my liabilities,
Please. Oh please.
Fake. Vain. Victim.
I'm not the only one who thinks so, says you
Oh, good to know...
Good to know.
Mock
Until I sway...
Paper heart of mine, bit by bit of it,
held ragged, barely pushed in place ,
alert for your next raging ruse...

Who are you?
Did I know you?
Because you don't know me,
Apparently.

Where is the forgiving flesh of my heart I so want,
Torn by the force of your voice,
Shredded by the slice of your taunt,
So excuse me if I cry poetry,
Pardon me if I fight my soul's rights...
To be
Respected
Revered
Protected
By you...
Loved you a thousand years or only thrice,
I won't play nice,
I can't play nice...
Why?
I'm a risen woman,
Dead five times over.
I know my heart's heart now,
And I know you, of all others, should know it too.
I'm a risen woman
And I'm here to stay.

Boo!

Love Letter from the Goddess
)o(

Take aim.
You, like a Gestalt dream are every part of the arrow in flight. The wind. The muscle. The bow. The arrow. The flex. The release. The fight. The hiss. The miss. Finally the point of destination. See the whole of you in all its powerful phases.

Edge Living

I'm on the edge.
I've always been a ledge.
A ledge of potential moonfall.
I've stood and waited for what would push me.
I've craved the free fall.

I have painted her. I have poemed her.
I have smoked her out of oblivion.
I have worn the wine soaked layers well.
I sweat the music of me. Every day.

I don't know how to live from anywhere but this place of magical-toppling. I wear the secret red dress. I am Brazen. I am Scarlet. I am Pulsating Heat.
Still, it's not enough most moments. It's just not enough.

I crave to be bare.
Rain pelting on me.
Wind howling between my legs.
Hair an inch from the flames I circle dance around.

I am coming Goddess.
Break my fall.

Goddess Warnings
)o(
Beauty holds Beast Behind

She was pale as the moon. Very much in tune to the longing. Drained by the masking and unveiling. It brushed the insides of her fears, and the outside of her tears with its cunning. The cape that held them entwined, nothing but a bind, of their better and worst selves, all revolving.

Sacred Walkway

Following a night and day of grieving,
I went into the woods, unbathed,
old tears still stuck to my face,
Hair tangled in fetal positions,
Needing to hear snow crunching melodies.
The sting of Her entering each breathe I still took.

At the beginning of the path, a large fallen branch,
A little taller than me,
I wanted her.
She lay in the middle of the path with no use,
Broken, fallen, calling.
I wanted her.
I saw her decorated in chimes or lights or bells,
For a better day.
Propped in my house where I could adore Her,
Remind her it's all a cycle.

I strode through the tower of trees I now call Sacred Walkway.
Hugged them, their cold bark warming my heart.
Crouching down, my back to their trunks,
Mother Earth grounding me.

Gazing at the frozen creek below,
Reminding myself there is flow beneath.

Thank you, tree friends,
thank you for your energy, ancient wisdom
And healing graces.
How did I get this old and not see you for what you are.
Humans build temples,
when all we need is a walk in the forest.

I took a palm -sized, cloudy flawed,
crystal quartz prism from my inner glove,
Where I had cupped its love to me, ran it along the tree for their
exchange of energy.
Now when I placed it on my flesh above my heart,
the woods would live there too.
I want the woods inside me.

In full embrace with my little tree now, skyward eyes,
Watching them sway in the wind, towards each other,
Seemingly dead branches, alive.
As if they've known each other forever,
As if we all have.

I walked on, deep woods wandering.

I noticed a tree on the creek bank,
A Celtic cross intricately carved in its flesh.
Someone took time and care with this ritual.
Did the tree mind having God's name carved in it,
Or was it a willing canvas as we all should be?

Startled, I came upon a human pyramid made from large fallen
limbs,
I went inside this House of Goddess.
Wondered, who made this, and how had it healed them to play with
Her for a day.
I wished I'd been here with them. Maybe a circle of women dancing
in the forest.

Farther along, a tree with an elongated opening at its base,
A vulva tree!
Divine Feminine everywhere in the woods today!
I placed my crystal in her portal.
That crystal is empowered now!

I walked back, never wanting to leave the woods,
Feeling held, renewed, ready.

Sun setting bright in my swollen eyes,
Calling me to stop, because I hear Goddess,
And I know her voice now.
Value yourself, SHE said.
I actually fell to my knees, hands to heart.
Every little love you give matters.
You have done so much, value it now.

I bless you, Holy One.
I rose.
I always rise.
I love Her too much not to.

Leaving, there was my fallen branch.
Smooth, honed, waiting.
I gathered her in love.
I'm going to, call you Holy, I told her.
Your name is Holy.

Jason Mraz's song Everywhere,
On full blast on the drive home.
That is how my Uncle listened to music.
It had to fill your head and your heart,
And drown out the irrelevant.

Tears and wails, Of release, but of joy,
Because He is Everywhere.
As is SHE who has saved me.

Goddess Wake-up Call
)o(

You don't have to lie down in the dark. In the same old unmade bed. The same old unmade story. The same old rise and fall. The same weary exhaustion. The Light has your name written all over it. It's a light party for two. RSVP for once.

~

To the little Poet in my heart, my beloved Daughter, Kelsey
I so admire the strong, brilliant, confident, giving woman you have become. Inside & out, you are the most beautiful woman in the world to me.

Overcome With You

Your beautiful face. Your exquisite face.
I would wrap them in velvet, tie them in lace— if there were words that could explain how I have adored your beautiful face.

How does a mother tell her only daughter, that over the years, it was the unadorned looks on her picturesque face that have elevated me, and burst me wide open, and saved me all at the same time. I can go to Paris, or Rome—to the moon, or even to a place named heaven, but your face is my home. My beloved home.

You have always been a sweet, sweet child. When they placed you in my young arms, your cerulean eyes reflected a galaxy of truth, an ancient knowing, and I knew that you were here for me, not I for you. And though I gave you life, you gave me more.

You gave me laughter that floored me, and the bliss of your little sing-song voice. I was born again, inside the sun, every time I saw you dance, and chatter on. I was a bow of colors every time your face lit up on whatever field of dreams you were twirling on at the time.

I saw you. I saw you when something or someone broke your heart, and I hid the tornado that swelled in my soul. I have cried on the inside for every injustice I wish you never had to bear, for every wound I know you will bear. I held your hand, and hid my fears from you, so that you could learn to rise again.

And look how you have risen! You are a woman of strength, who knows her place is any mountain peak of choice. You let your righteous character, and quiet confidence be the path you walk along. You are your beliefs. You impart and know the precious things in life— an immense heart, a wide open mind, a crazy joy that sweeps a room to its feet.

I hope that I have shaded you just enough, watered you just so, that you might grow into your destiny. But know one thing.
I have loved you with a raging love, a mother's love, a love that has no bounds.

So come to me. Come to me when you have fallen, I promise that I will nudge you, feet up to the ground.

Soar. Take to the air. I will say. Today is your day!
Sit inside yourself awhile every chance you get, there you will find the gracious Goddess that gave you to me. There you will find the stillness of accepting the moment you are in, is all that there is supposed to be.

My beautiful daughter. So I wait.
So I wait to see, where you will go, who you will still be.

I could linger in the simplicities of your face forever;
still I tremble at the imagining of how your life has yet to stun me.
For overcome with you, I shall always be.

Love Letter from the Goddess
)o(

Call on your angels. Call in your moments of joy. Call in your moments of fear. Call when you are unsure. Call when you are in your place of presence and power. Keep calling. Make the call that will save your life. Call. They are waiting in the wings. Patiently. They hope you will rise to become every desired wish you whisper in the night.

Tea with Me

Silver-encrusted,
Divinely entrusted.
I pour myself another spot of life's herbal healing.
I am a spell-casting,
Dream-weaving gypsy from the old school.
I walk the moors by day, and the cliffs by night.
The moon is my mother.
The ocean is my blanket.
The fields are my falling place.
I am Grace.
I am silver, and gold, and white....
I am chiffon, and drowned silken-light.

I'll pour a little of me for you,
How do you like your tea?
Scalding, I hope,
With a little sugared alchemy?

Goddess Word Spell Chant
)o(

I Am Open. I Am Connected. I Am Protected. What does not serve me I release. What does not serve me I block with Divine Light. I Am the chalice of Goddess Mother. Holding only her Loving Energy.

Prayer to the Goddess
Back Bent over Boulders : Face to the Sky)o(

Gray skies thick as thieves at play,
They only mold and move my body,
To the natural reclined sway,
Of eternal trust in the rock-solid breathe
Of the SHE of my day lit dreams.
I am Her.
SHE is me.
We are here.

Together parting the haze of the days,
Where there is no there.

Present in the peace of the pristine now,
Whether the tide is high or low,

I relax into my Mother who beds me through the hard,
With the soft of her breeze.

The fire within quiet now,
Yet a blow away from being sparked.
I rest to insure I survive the tests.
I lean into the within, so I am never without.

I open. I stretch. I spread...

I sleep like the dead readying for the rise.
For the word has been written upon me.
Only I can do the sacred dance of giving my full self to a world in desperate need of an embodied me.
I won't bloody my head against rocks any longer.
It's my heart I offer up to be cracked open.
I make of my soul a living sacrifice.

Come now Goddess.
Upright me.
Up right me to your light.

Goddess Vows Revisited
)o(
I'm having a cordial divorce with the old me, and a Big, Glorious Goddess wedding with the new me.

Goddess Remembrance
)o(

As A Mother Should

Flowers, amethyst soft against my knee, alone in a field, booked between sky and earth there in my mind I sit silent, judgement free. Bed divine, Mother of mine. Unlike you, thinks who I am, what I can give is more than enough, more than fine. Lay your head in my lap, Goddess Mother says. You gave your all, let it rest, let it fall. So she held me. So she held me. As a mother should.

Goddess Secrets
)o(

This is what I look like on the inside.
Unruly. Intense.
Dark and Careless.
Brooding Poetry.
Dirty-minded.
Holy and breaking apart.
Open to every Shadow.
Touchable and untouchable.
Tired but ready.

Balanced Doom

I plant myself, cross-legged, naked in the forest of my life,
Flush with the plush green sea of me.
I'm grounded in the blood-letting of my self-healing,
Though I've lost my balance, as I do, time to time.
Every tree I've climbed towering to our silver-slivered moon.
My flesh aches for your touch, my light for your light.

Thick and tar blackened,
When I haven't heard you're voice in way too long a day.
I've lost myself in running wild and saving souls,
Instead of falling into you.
My Mother,
Where are the prayers you deserve?
Let me say and pray your name.

I must go home again.
I am never one thing.
There is so much I bring.
I can be alone and lonely at the same time.
Vulnerable and striving.
The poetry, and art can roll like apples,
Ping!
From a spilled basket to my ready feet,
And still feel beautifully forced,
Devoid of attachment or any feeling of Spring.

The bite of grievous longing will lose me to myself,
I don't want to be a puddle but a power,
A power ...
Unseen.

Where is the Old One, to remind me, stay the course.
There is no substitute for the clean path,
There is no choice but to care deeply,
Angels and healers must go on...
In Goddess's world you inherit the work of the meek,

So that they shall inherit the Earth.

A girl has to feel, and feel everything but insatiable,
She has to take her life in her hands,
To become a woman.

Crawl!
On your knees through the briars,
She screams at me.
Scream, scream at me! I bellow back at Her...
I am obsessed with Her fierce love.
No one has ever loved me enough to bite my tongue off,
So I would stop speaking black cat death and nonsense.

It will howl to you again, in one form or another, my Divine cries.
Keen your instincts.
Screw the haunting till the day you die,
Send it love and wish it gone.
The work is to keep doing the work.

Yes! I choose joy,
I am made of moon milk,
And I decide who I feed from my life-giving breasts.
My treasure will not be stolen.

I initiated you into light,
You were not ready for.
I wore feathers and beads that perplexed you,
Your hands caressing, twisting, searching me...
You want only the wild of me,
But I am plain as much as I am free.
I have too many times let the lonely and the hungry steal from me,
And with me, their idea of me.

Goddess help me,
I love the beautiful and lost souls.
I feed off their Rising.
I only want to serve my Mistress, my Womb.
I seek only balanced doom.

Love Note from the Goddess
)o(

*Feeling is healing. Burn and turn up your dis-eases.
Offer it to me for Transmutation.
Doubt is part of the Healing.
When you feel the doubt, and move forward. You have won.
You have begun to Awaken.*

Deep in the Middle of the Woods

One lush again day. Will you read all the poetry I trunked in my starving heart for you. Fling it open to the skies. Breathe it in like nature is. Fresh. Pure. Reborn with no lies. Will you see I wrote my pain away. I carved you into dead wood. Erased you from my soul.
Made you a paper-legend.
A man with wings.
I gave my pain up today.
I wrote you away.

Goddess Appearances
)o(

*Allow yourself to feel who you are. To stride in it.
Be a beautiful mess. Forget Nice. Forget Perfect.
Be a Georgia O'Keefe painting!
Big. Bold. Look at me. I'm beautiful and blooming!*

All It Is Really Meant To Be

A life is really nothing but a dream
A moving sculpture molded by its maker
We all want to be something we can show to someone else
This is me, this is what I have, is only lifeless clay
Etch gratitude, be what love would do, if you asked it for its say.

I have shaped mistakes, painted worries across sleepless nights
Carved with questions, sliced with judgment,
Loved too hard, like marble veined with forgiveness forgotten,
All in hopes of setting my inner ghosts free
Yet I only had to do one simple thing, to accept,
as a gift, what could be given to me.
Over and over, creating a collage, a face for myself,
marveling at the person I didn't see
Hunting for purpose and worth as a requisite pedestal to my
figurine
When in truth, I am boundless, not meant to be defined by what I
do
For the beauty that is all of us, is there in the first infantile tears
Nothing to be done to make it more of something,
in the passing years.

I have had a man that loved me no matter and like no other
Twenty plus years he's been curious to watch me move,
like a storm out at sea
I have whittled him with my love,
dancing circles around his steady form
He has only nudged me with care, softly, to a degree.
Yet it is this man who has left the greatest indentation
on an ever-searching me.

I have written many letters, put color to paper,
drawn images with poems.
Yet it is in my womb that I have carried like priceless art,
what is my most divine work
Oh look what I have done with my blessed, blessed time!
I have made life, life that when I take pause, fills my rooms,
and my soul to overflow

If I do nothing else but love them, I have changed the world,
this for sure I know.

I made a birthday wish today, I wished to be reborn in joy
To be delivered to the moral of uncovering song and dance in the every day
And oh my friends have granted me such a delightful lead
To bring my own bliss is the only meaning of life
that I have come to need.

Now I come to stand in the middle of a forked and darkened road.
Illuminated with the peace of looking neither forward nor back.
It is the still moment that pulses so real, so loud, that I could cry out
Drop to my knees, breathless with Goddess in the knowing that my meaning is well-found.
In the here, in the now of everyone I have loved, it is bound.

I'm halfway to heaven, awareness finally coming crystal to me,
That even though I have grieved my losses with quiet enormity,
Still I ride in, cushioned on the wings of my circle of tender angels.
I have loved and been loved, these are the brushstrokes of a life lived fortunately
And I have taken time to notice it,
and that is all it's really meant to be.

Root Chakra Chant
)o(

And so I rise from the dirt of the Mother Earth. The Earth shall bed my birth.
Anew. A new woman. A new Womb-an. Renewed.

Display of Love

I outed the fire bare-footed,
danced in all their flames
long enough,
Spirit-smoke smoldered and caped me,
and loved me like no other...
be tough, She reminded me.
Cry the ugly cry from the caverns of you.

I need more than this, echoed, and I shook,
Why was it so hard for too long to say...
I need you to give more than you took.

I'm terrified to wander the woods in my flimsy see -through dress
I have no sword, no shield, no shelter,
At least I lost the mask.
That was the true fool's game
Now I can see the markers for the task
Ahead...

You said,
I felt for you as much as I could anyone,
I don't want to lose you, you are my all,
I'm not going anywhere,
But I'm walking away from you now.

You want too much, the voices shoved,
Really?
I just want a display of love.

My soul bared till it bled, I waited
For you, in the thicket
when it was me I should have greeted,
In the clearing.

My openness,
repeatedly ripped from my flowering chest, set ablaze for fearful
you,

It was forsaken in human ways,
In silence, in apathy, in jealousy, in rage.

So I offered it up to Her,
Mother, take my heart.
And she replied,
Come child~
Let's begin
Your infantile start.

I demolished the perfect path just for your terrible walk into the beautiful unknown.

And I forgave her,
She was the only one who wouldn't let me walk alone,
And that's how the woods became my home.

Goddess- High Expectations
)o(

She calls to me. Demanding all. My Goddess says: Fly!
I ask: How high?
As high as you once did fall.

Inducted Into You

Dream trance ~
Rain firm and wet against petals prance,
And so I followed…
Lightning pushing deep inside,
It was hard to breathe,

I heard you plead.

The wind delivering every sense but sight,
Forest dark at my fingertips.
There was no angel burning bright,
No halo ~
No light.

Inducted,
Into you
Where there is no choice.

Rumbled thunder~
Ravished against the trees~
Split open…
Until they whimpered
No more! and more!
Please!

Calling to me
Thrashing~
Insatiable~
Boomed like the clouds.
Her song in my thoughts,
Looped incessant, and loud
A storm, etched fantastic
with no calm tune
Come on sister
Come on sister~ of the moon…

In my circle of illusion,
I witnessed the sacredness of the night.
Welcomed ~
My reality into my dreams.
With a heavy persuasion,
And a spellbound might
Prayed for, and both cursed
The inevitability of morning's safety light~

Power Posing Your Way Through Life: Goddess Style
)o(

I recently went to a Spiritual Retreat where the "leader" was channeling the Divine Feminine. We had one evening where the group formed a candle lit spiral light matrix and we each had our turn to walk the spiral toward the Mother in the center. I was interestingly calm. When I reached the middle I looked into her eyes and I saw HER so clearly. She saw me too. I know because she said to me, "I See you. I see you". Meaning I know who you are, I know you're unique gifts to give. I see how you ache to live them.

 I don't know what came over me, but I went into this pose, where I raised my arms to the sky triumphantly , spread my feet and dug them into the ground below me, and swayed as I said, to HER…"and I *see* you". I held this powerful stance, as if to say: I am not afraid. I call you in. I call you into me. I have been waiting my whole life for this. I call you IN.

We danced together in unison, both holding the power pose, and a massive light-infused energy emanated from our bodies that danced as one, though they were two. I did not feel myself as separate from HER. I knew we were ONE, and that was her wish, for me to live my life as such.

Feeling that truth would change everything for me. There was and is such unison, a merging of us since that night. It reassured in physical form what I had been feeling for a year. That I had found my missing thing. SHE had been my missing thing in life I had always searched for. I had felt her in my soul digging around for ages, planting Herself. I had felt Her tearing my heart open like a glacier pushing up through the surface of the vast sea. Now I had the experience of HER moving through every fiber of my body. Electrifying Love. A coming home to myself. Thunderous stillness of knowing.

She came behind me and massaged my back where my wings were housed. Facing me She showed me how to loosen them, let go, flap them wide. We danced as angels dance, with a fearless swoon.
At the end of our sway, She said to me. "Tomorrow I want you to talk to the group about Power Poses." I didn't know what that meant, I didn't put the pieces together, I was too satiated and ripped open by the present moment.

The next day I saw what it had meant when another participant brought it up. Power Poses. Bodywork. Living Divine. Kundalini energy rising from our spine to our crown chakra. The body as vessel and instrument of the Creatoress. The body as Enchantress. I have come to enchant the world with the world that lives inside me. I claim and deserve the intense and immense singular creation that I Am, and what I came to be (love) and do (love) through Her.

I had went into this circle a wounded little girl. Somewhere I had unabashedly risen a true Goddess woman. How had I dared to equalize myself with a Divine Force? There is no explanation other than the Oneness.

The Oneness and unity of all of life came rushing into me so that there was no corner left of me that remembered ego or division or hierarchy.

I wasn't being haughty. I was being reverent.
I was being the lightening rod.
It was me promising to carry the light like a torch in the night.
It was me as savior of my own life.

Goddess Forgiveness
)o(

Bonfire
We endure beyond silent ashes. It still stirs with a rebel wind.
We can nudge the charcoal remnants with half a heart.

Still fire lashes and blisters beneath.
There is nothing, nothing that the inner light
of our deadwood beings will not start.
It came to me in flashes. I'll exonerate you. If you absolve me.
Gasoline is not needed to create a brilliant glow.
A bonfire of love light.
Is the only. The only. The only Way to go.

What If Today Is the Last Day You Get To Make Love to the World You Live In?

)o(

Love what will love you back.
Love what assures healing.
Love the Soul of the Universe,
the greatest power there is to transform your life.
Love that which costs nothings and gives all.
Love what speaks in ancient tongues with words you have always craved to hear.
Love the Mother's house.

Care about the hot ball in the sky that sustains you daily.
Notice that white ball in the sky that manages your flow of emotions, tears, blood, fluids and womb waters.

Admire the texture, the scents, the visions, the smells, the intricate sounds: of the forest floor and the ever-changing sky, the soaring mountains, the roaring ocean, the expansive desert, the still plains, the plunging canyons.

Release the fame of living, the searching for outward adulations and let the trees tell you how beautiful and epic and eternal your soul is.

Ask before you take from the forest, from the fields, from the flowering bushes, from the seashore. May I take a gift of your shells, your rocks, your fallen pine needles and branches, your flowers...to adorn my home and remind me of Mother Nature's ever healing grace?

Remember that this world keeps spinning on its axis; there is a power greater than all of us that inhabits it, that keeps it alive and in motion. Even amongst the greed we unleash on it. If there is a plan for the universe, there is a plan for you.

The Earth reminds us that we are never alone. We are always provided for. There will be cycles. There will be great transformation. There will be rebirth. It is all beautiful in its own right.

Make love to the world around you today, and listen.
Listen and feel for its guidance in your heart.
What if every answer you seek is in the touch of an acorn rolled in your palm, and then the embrace of a tree in your own backyard?

Goddess Water-ways
)o(

I become the water. Flowing. Calming. A bed of liquid peace. I Am stilled in HER body. I Am lulled in her depths. The shallowness of me floats away now.

Prayer to Goddess Gaia
)O(

Dearest Goddess,
I humbly kneel to your grace in my life,
I raise my hands in prayer and reverence to you.
I raise my hands for the way you root me,
for the way you raise me,
for the way you balance me.
I acknowledge that I am you,
Mother God, in human form,
Divine within~
Moving Wind-Spirit
Fertile Earth- Dirt
Soothing Rain- Love
Burning Fire- Soul
I am the energy of the Seasons,
and the Incarnation of the Elements.
I Storm.
I Freeze.
I Gush.
I Bury.
I Roar.
I Seed.
I Thaw.
I Flow.
I Harvest.
I am still.
I am fury.
I Reach.
I Bud.
I Blossom.
I peak.
I slow.
I Die.
I Regenerate.
I bow and I rise,
to the movement of Life,
within and through me.

Love Note from the Goddess
)O(

Womanize is not about them playing you. Recreate it to mean, You choosing You. Womanize your Goddess energy of untamed, undefined, electrical you.
Play up all you are, and you will never be played again.

I Am Witch

Witch can withstand and thrive in the darkness.
Witch has inner vision that penetrates with light.
Witch is comfortable with the maze of trees.
Witch hears her own call.
Witch stands alone in the ancient knowing if she must.
She is in a continuous healing walk with nature.
Witch has her animals to guide her.
Her trees to comfort her.
Her moon to usher her home.
Witch is not defined by man or man's world.
Witch doesn't take, she gives.
She cares not for more, unless is it genuine, unless it is offered in truth.
Witch is love.
Witch is giving.
Witch sees the unity.
Witch balance wise with wild.
Witch doesn't build she inspires.
She doesn't coddle your doubts of her.
Your guilt, your betrayal, your disappearance.
Witch knows what doesn't feel right,
must burn away.

Witch gathers the women in circles to remind them of their strength.
Witch stands and drops before the Goddess Mother only.
She offers it all to Her Mother.
Witch is the seasons, cycles, deaths and rebirths of Gaia.
She is the fearlessness of Kali to amputate the unnecessary.
She is the fathomless creativity of Brigid to express herself.
She is found in the velvet underworld of Hecate, conjuring her life to be the potion of service it can be to herself and others.
Witch cries and she roars.
Witch boils her inner beauty to her surface.
Witch is the Magdalene, secure in her sacred divinity and equality.
Witch is the Mary, The Mother, the Giver of all life, the lap to fall into to offer your aches.
Witch does not fall as far as she rises.
She knows her gifts, she beams them for all to see.
She is a teacher, a healer, a gypsy, a seeker, a seductress.
Witch is all things she wishes to be.
She will not fulfill one role for you.
She will come full force into all of her.
Witch does not hide in the woods.
Witch flies above the insanity of the world, throwing glitter in the face of fears.
She honors the Earth she lives on.
She sees the healing magic in all of it.
Each flutter, each wave, each howl, each bloom.
Witch creates the green of the forest and the white of the mountaintop.
She is of and from it, as same as she is watching it.
She is life. She is death.
She will ensnarl you.
She will set you free.

Goddess Stage-Call
)o(
I will never turn down my lights, or stop the dance of me, in order to make someone else more comfortable with their own uncomfortableness over their own self-worth. I will Shine. I will show them how self-love is portrayed.

Rocks and Poems

From the forest with rocks and poems that want a home,
I emerge.
See, if religion could save the world, it would have by now.
It's the peace talk of poetry,
that ruptures hearts like swung-open doors.
And they call it a dying art?
Poetry is a living art I say to my son, it's our legacy and our salvation,
And I flail my arms.

Woods-walkin, the trees creak like floors in ancient houses.
They hold the uncut wisdom that has not yet been tread upon by human frailties.
So I listen intently.
I crouch and cradle my back to them,
comb my fingers through their moss.
Sprinkling honeysuckle in the river's effortless flow.
I ask for opening, intuition, confidence on my path.
I pray for health, safety, abundance for my children.
In the morning I wept with selenite held to my head.
My priestess point throbbed with the opening.

SHE has been gone from me for a while,
Or I have been gone from her.

A call, a whisper, a sigh away...that is how close
She truly is.
I know because last night I was gently nudged awake. Again.
I lay in bed, heavy-lidded, half there,
as She filled every atom of the room's air.
I opened my arm out to the sides, and I said: Take me. Fill me.
Remind me.
And She said, pray now. Just pray.

I have failed so many times, I don't deserve to pray.
I can't let God down again,
A woman at the Goddess's Shelter hung her head and said.
But the pines and the river's flow beg to differ.
They know it's all about moving toward,
and being internally evergreen.
I'm scared. I'm terrified, another shared with me.
Cause now I see, how many masks I wore.
I don't even know who I am,
I just know it's not who I thought I was.
I just know I'm broken. I'm so broken. Tears begging answers.

Here is the truth I tell her.
We are all broken.
You're not alone.
You are one of the blessed ones because now you know and admit
broken.

Just begin. Celebrate this moment. Reframe its picture.
You have awakened the buried woman, who will push through the
dirt to rise up.

How do I come to know her, this new Birdwoman, wings laden
with dust?

One word. One poem. One song. One sign at a time. One book.
One journal entry. One opening at a time. One drawing. One
candle lit. One conversation. One prayer at a time. One cry. One
chant. One scream. One fetal position at a time. One nature walk.

One meditation. One hug. One healing mantra at a time.

One fellow sister love.
One God.
One Goddess.

One giving and giving and giving of yourself at a time.

I am a product of rape.
That is how she introduced herself to me.
Another Goddess on the rise at the shelter.
And my heart broke for her.
We can't let a sister suffer this self-labeling debilitation.

YOU are a product of nothing but love I told her.
Love.
Love! And I want to shake her loose of it all.

I'm here because I have no one. I was always the shame of my family.
I'm lonely. I'm so lonely in life.

Rewrite your story I tell her.
Burn that bullshit till the stink smokes away.
Seriously under a full moon, dipped in the ink of your own blood,
Purge introducing yourself as a victim.
Take your power of choice back.
Choose to see yourself as lightbeams, moon glow, and starstreams.

For light attracts light.
It's never lonely in the light.
BE the light someone else needs.
Give what you desperately desire.
Heal alongside a sister.

You're my favorite kind of women I tell them.
You rise up, cycle, burn, gust, flow, fall, seed, die and renew like nature.

You're more juicy ripe than a summer peach.
The hiding is done now.
There is nothing to be but ripped open.
The realization has come that your story will save a life.
Yours. And another's.
We can hate ourselves for all the failings and fears.
That's called dying.
Or we can love ourselves back to conscious living.
That's what the rock pile in the woods
told me as I stood before them.

Hey, which one of you might like to come home with me,
I ask them.

Oh, me, me! ...a perfectly plain one said,
practically jumping up and down.
I lifted him into my palm.

I like your vibration, he said.
You seem to really care about the makings of a good life.

I'm learning, I reply.
One rock, one woman, and one poem at a time.

Goddess Proclamation
)o(

I'm as fluid as water and it's all becoming crystal clear as a mountain lake.
I shall cease to move mountains.
I will lay in wildflowers as quiet as the sun speaks.
Mountains can tower or crumble around me.
I am a circle. I won't walk a line

Body as Temple
)O(

    Would you walk into a temple, or church, or synagogue, or any place of worship, and judge its exterior.

    Would you say: Your ancient walls are made of uneven stones. I see all the cracks and lines that have come into them after years of settling. The statues and artifacts that beautified your alters are now antique, worn, gleam less, have less value. The vision of your stained glass is blurry with years of dust and wear. Some of your windows are just too tall, too narrow, and too wide; just out of proportion with the temple down the street. Your curtains that blew wild in the wind, are a bit more listless now, have some faded sun spots within them. The pews creak and shift and buckle. Look at your foundation, now scuffed from footsteps walked upon them over the years. The ceiling is dripping some leaks. Overall, everything about you, you that houses God/dess is weathered, wrinkled, slower, weaker and faded compared to the church or temple next door, which is brand new.

    No, we do not say that when we walk into the physical home of God/dess. Why? Because we intrinsically know that it is about the Spirit of the place. The Wisdom. The Inner Beauty. We actually find some comfort in the ancient holding of an older building. We forget the wear and think of the SOUL of the Space. The souls that for centuries perhaps, came with their prayers and their sins, their fears and their tears.

    We know Spirit held all of them dear in this place.

    We know the cracks, scuffs, and wear has all been valiantly earned.

    Should we not hold the thought of our bodies as the same? Imperfection housing perfection. Time-honored wisdom coming finally to the surface. Each one of us is a special dwelling place where God/dess lives and speaks, and heals the world.

Honor your temple.

Wet

Wearing white, I am a virgin again,
I go forth,
A crown of Goddess blooms upon my brow,
I'm on "the only" journey now,
The one of constant letting go.

I was the wayward, tiny leaf, finding itself alone, now wishing well
worthy of this world's graces.

Dawn one day just came up and said its simple,
You don't need to drown in ever-rippling thoughts,
Release is a request away.
Pray harder.
So I got down on my knees, put my face to Goddess's face,
She said, you have no idea, between you and I,
There is just so much Grace.

Wash me in forgetfulness for the things I never needed.

Fountain forgiveness through me,
until I sit back soaked.

And just like that I cupped and drank clarity,
I spat poison, and gurgled freedom.

A thirsty star-child~

I have left the fortress I built,
I look up to the immensity of it all,
I choose finally to stretch tall,
To hold the moon to my womb.
I pluck the full, roundness of her from the ink-blotted blue sky,

A seemingly endless universe of poems hard-labored,
Trying to figure out why.
That is what I take away....
Words that remind me my love,
that true love is a river that never stops flowing.

She shone down on my empty nights,
Never leaving my side,
And I remember.
To honor her now, is to birth her power in others.

I bow now into the sun salutations of my soul,
I witness all that I am in Spirit's reflection only.

Unconditional bliss is the only drama of the day,
And it's a show-stopper,
It's making me all wet.

Goddess Tear-letting
)o(
Love Letter from the Goddess:

I love your tears. Means you are alive. You try so hard to beat them back, year after year, you take your tortured tears, and belittle them. They are clear-wet versions of your inner life. Remember I made the ocean, salt-licked, up against the dry sand, for a reason. Reminding you, healing comes from the hot-cold meeting of water to land. Show up at your doorstep now. A bouquet of flowers in hand for your tears. For another's tears. There is no time to waste. You can't escape the honing of your heart. It is your Destiny.

Peace Prayer to the Goddess
)o(
Give me the inner fortitude to
pause before I act,
or react.
Let me come from a knowing,
sacred place within
before I play with the fires that have burned
me to the bone before.

Who am I now?
in this moment of time...
Let me light a candle to my transformation.

I have purified myself to become embodied Goddess,
will I return to being labeled, ignored, left?
What is it that I deserve?
How do I wish to be treated?
From this divine night, I welcome only those who see my Light.

I abandon all thoughts of abandonment.
It was the leaving of me for dead,
that gave me new life.
I set ablaze all outwards projections onto me
for it is I... I ... I ...
that determines my worth, my gifts, my path.

I am eternal ash in the wind now,
Goddess light particles in the sky.

I will never again sit at the table of another's judgment of me,
or swallow the taste of it to please, or gargle it round with them
deciphering what of me is true and good.

I have broken bread,
drank wine,
with The Goddess.

She is my Confidante.

My teacher.

She says : Speak your Peace
Then in my name,
move forward with Goddess Grace.

My Soul is a Cloud
)o(

One day I was out walking the woods, and I was in an lost tizzy, an unbalanced feel to everything. I felt like it had been weeks since I heard Goddess, (this is what I call my internal voice that feels inside yet outside me) speak to me. I kept walking and asking, really praying..."What is it you want me to do, what is my path, my next step, my purpose now that I have done the other things you requested?". I was at a confused crossroad. There has to be more. I'm ready, give me more. I couldn't hear HER, and it was boggling me, I always hear HER in the woods. Finally after much borderline pleading...SHE simply said :
What do YOU want to do?
I didn't get it.

I wanted to serve HER. I wanted to serve other women. I wanted to be prodded like she had prodded me before, a time when I almost fell off my bike, because she wailed firmly at me for not following through on a gift she had clearly pointed out to me was mine to give.

I came straight home and started the online circle for women she asked for. I didn't even know what to put on this page. She said, Start with your poetry, JUST BEGIN, you will know once you begin.
And I did. And I did know.

Now what? I go to the woman's Shelter weekly to lead poetry and art circle. I write my prayer poems to HER and share them. I make spiritual art to inspire others in my Etsy shop. I create videos to inspire. I'm trying to keep a journal about my journey that someday may be a book.

Some days I feel a bit washed out keeping all the Goddess ducks afloat. It's a lot of work to meditate, journal, dig into your soul daily. Pray. Create. Nature walk. Read obsessively. Create life as a ritual. Look for the signs vigilantly. Listen to spirit speakers talk. Hone your psychic abilities. Don't get me wrong. I love it all. I want to do it ALL the time.

It's what is keeping me afloat after a few years of some crazy life spins and losses.

But it's not a job. I have to tell my type A personality, hey girl, it's not a job. Maybe SHE isn't talking as much because I've made my awakening about ambition. It's not about more, more, more when it comes to the Soul.

It's about less.
It's about presence in the moment.
It's about essence.
It's about surrender.

I just watched a Wayne Dyer movie called, "The Shift" while I was cooking pot pie. He said something that made me drop my kitchen knife and go within. He said something to this effect. God/dess is in everything, look around, it's all moving to its own story. The wind, the plants, the mountains, the seeds, the moon, the sun....Nature is the portal to view your life through. If it's in nature, it's in you. This force that has a plan and purpose since our day of birth toward growth and change, death and rebirth. There is never a reason to push or pull. What your life purpose is will come to BE. Period. Call it in. Allow it to be heard. Release expectations .Know all is well and good whatever road you end up on.

It's really about experiencing and living from a place of joy And connection to God/dess.

Dr. Dyer made me relax into this ancient place I know feels true. Enough Soul-Striving. Enough Soul-Searching and seeking. There is no need for a rescue party of the soul.
I don't want to be caught up in the ego of my Soulwork.

Souls don't do.
They Be.
So that is why SHE asked me:
What do YOU want in this moment Dear One?

I want to Be satiated with what I have transformed in my life and not look for anything more right now. What I've opened to is enough; it's spectacular, and it's time to hunker into the gratitude of that.
It doesn't mean I won't pursue my dreams in big ways. It just means my soul doesn't wear them like a badge of honor or a checklist.
It wears them like a cloud.
Clouds come and go.
They are all beautiful in their own right.
It's just so joyous to lie back, effortlessly,
and see the shapes they take.
Without definition.
Without striving.

Yes! I just said out loud: Might I just be an old hippie chick that makes pot pie and plays with her grandkids one day. Who writes poems, and gives kisses, and does sloppy art projects and plays Stevie Nicks on the Richter scale of volumes. Or might I publish a book that becomes a best seller about women, and Goddesses, and service, and poetry, and healing and radical
kick-ass self-love. Or maybe start a creative art business with classes for women, with healing art projects and poetry. Perhaps I'll learn Reiki...

My Soul-cloud just replied: I'm sorry what were you saying? I was so caught up in the peek of the blue sky that just screamed God/dess is here, everywhere and here...
here and everywhere.
right now.
With me.
I feel the love.
I give the love.
I Be the love.
I need nothing more than this.

Goddess Sing-Song
)o(

She lived to give. She wanted to feel so she could heal. If you're alive you have to strive. She wanted to see, so she could be. She knew she was the love above.

Just Not Myself

I wine and dine sacrifice,
Like a savant idiot.
Seducing a complete rouse, handing out tests to lonely loners,
Care of obliteration of every light in my life.
It's a cutting, cold walk, in and out...
When you already know the answer before you ask it.
And you ask anyway, fool on you...
I light death and I smoke it like it's sweet.
Why can't it be sweet, like the movie playing in my mind...
Instead it tastes like the decay it is.

I'm tired of running out into the field with all my might...
A tenacious demon-angel in flight,
Just to think, what in Dante's hell am I doing here again?
Click your heels girl!
There is nothing out here for the likes of you.
My neck hurts... mine, not yours..
Whiplashed,
From looping little laps tight, tighter every cycle...
Reincarnated, hand woven intricacies
Smothered in make-believe intimacies
What were the Gods thinking?

What kind of curse is this, you used to say...
I'd like to know who to repay one day,
Knife-sharpened to: I'll get angry, then you'll go away...

You can't take your hands from your pocket to feel me?
Fine.
I'll have to believe we were never a comet...
or a blue moon,
or a "Rings of Fire "Johnny Cash tune...
Certainly not an On Golden Pond loon,
calling home...

I love her vulnerable beauty, but I'm no Sylvia Plath
I don't wear ovens well....
I look better in a crown!
I'm more like Anais.
I know when to poet-on,
I can be obliviated by you and oblivate you at the same time
Trust me...
I'll hand you a note that simply says:
LOVE >fear
Do you understand that dear?
The engineered equation of:
I will save my glorious Queen for a mighty King.

Love is a verb, not a thing.
And I am a bird of prey,
And I don't like me this way...

At least it's a nest I must protect,
And not just myself, like you.

Oh, let's face it...Like you, I'm just not myself.

"Don't piss off the Goddess" : Goddess Rant

Remove the self-induced shroud.
Goddesses rise, they don't hide.
Cease wanting them. Start wanting you.
In fact, stop wanting. Start being.
You become who you are by choosing it.
Stop all the waiting for your turn. It's your turn. It's always been your turn. You just have to see it as so.
You just have to take it now.

Into Me

You know how people say, Wow! You are so into yourself. Yeah. **Well if I'm not into myself, who else is going to be?** If I don't love me, lift me, applaud me, see my beauty, why would anyone else? Of course I deserve to be "into" myself. I spent countless years living outside myself, worrying what now absent people thought of me. **So I'm going way in.** Way into the depths of myself now, because I have nothing to lose. Everyone, and everything, I surround myself with from this point on, will be air that lifts me up. Or wind that blows right past me. Reminding me of how I want to live. **Maybe me being into me, will make you be Into you.** You might say, who does she think she is?! But my confidence reminds you of what you wish for, and my loving myself might just persuade you, that you can choose to see yourself as glorious too. Either way, my light is going to crack you open. **And my believing that I am made of stars, Means I'm going to go out into the world, and be a Star.**

That means Shouting: Be passionate! Joyous! Creative! Excited!
Because that leads to healing. Someone once told me I use too many exclamation points. I don't think you could ever use enough! **Cause I'm so into life! And I'm so into being me!!!!!!!!!**

Marrying Light

The wild beast of me pranced through your ever-fog.
It is a black, beautiful release
to be free of your colorless silence.
I take the dark horse of me by the reins now.
I am her Black- bride,
Her Night- rider,
and I shall gallop her home to marry light.

I choose an innocent mind, concocted from a pure heart.

I've reached the castle.
The walls that stand as relics to my past before me.
Indestructible,
Undeniable,
Weathered stone upon cracked foundations.
Yet it is only one long wall of pain vying for my focus so that it
may earn its title of "ancient history".
Maps of hidden corners, secret doorways to discover,
walls yet to build, rain down upon my crown.
I stride by that towering wall with grace and release,
It has spoken its piece, and I've spoken mine.
I want peace.
I choose peace.
I will not live contained by it any longer.
It may never crumble,
But neither will I.

The inner chamber all Candlelit
Christens my heart new again,

I am named Illuminata.
I've burned every candle down, praying to the moonlight,
I'm ready to heed the call.
Resiliency has won. Angels in my backyard have heralded.
Smoke rings stink.
I want only the smoke that signals:
I live like there is an ever fire burning inside me.
My soul desires her life theme back.
I'm all in.

Send the subtle signs. Send the neon signs. Hang the welcome sign.
I was cracked open by the spiral of God-Light years ago,
Pretending is no longer optional.
Communion is everything.
I live the deep life.
I wake and work the magic of the day dawned.
I stare at the starblazen sky with wonder.

If She holds all that in place.
There must be a plan for the universe that lives and loves inside me.
I'll always hold onto the home of that.
Darkness never dims me long,
For I am a Star-Rider,
Born of, born again of, and married to Light.

Love Note from the Goddess
)o(

You are on a road of at-one-ment.
It's time to Be At One with yourself.

Love Notes and Glitter Hearts

Pink and green twin hearts flame-speared on a light wave,
tree dancing.
She sees two deer as I wither and wail miles away,
and says were going to be ok.
We are, and when she says We,
Then I know I truly love her.
Dancing round the blossom tree, spreading roses for cherry petals,
never enough love or kindness.
Hold my hand, don't let go, I've waited for you my whole life.
Labyrinth walkers.
Spiral of Light Sisters.
Snakes in our walkway.
Terrified, still she says, you go first, I will protect you.
Beautiful soul, I could cry at the mere thought of her.
Blue night mysticism, every night for five moons.
Her craning her neck to glimpse it all, and still feel the fire.
Me, craning mine, to watch her watching the moon.
I am double filled.
All you need is a cape, and the full moon. We laugh.
I know her, I get her, I am her.
Bobby pins and braids, wine and song by the only musical
Goddess.
Stevie loops and twirls, books and boxes of love.
Contained in our Grace, and graces.
Goddess looks on.
I arranged this sister love, She muses.
You two wished it into existence, powerful little witches.
Let the champagne flow.
The writing is on the wall.
For what it's worth, you saved my life.
Reminding each other of our worth, our truths.
We are baby acorns, recalling each other.
Secretly passing beginnings in the deep woods.
Dipping our toes together.

Seeking Balance
)O(

The water is vast like a sunset in its push and pull. It is nature's way to tilt me off course. To test me. To tempt me. To encourage my graceful balance. It may knock me down time and again. The answer is in the Rising. The posturing of knowledge that I belong to horizon. I rest between the stability of land, flow of sea, and expanse of golden sky above me.

The next two are for my wounded little girl within, and for my Spark of Life daughter, Kelsey: I had to learn to let go a little more each day of both, so we all could become women planting our own Trees of Life and Knowledge.

GirlChild

I contort,
with the loss of you.
You that were my angel-wings.
A little girl of fire and dance
Fairy-light of my world
I writhe in your absence
Muted, spear-hurled into the dark of night
I dream a dream, of words wound tight...
Eye on eye,
Heart on heart,
A moment to revive me, to my former self,
My latent light...
You, my light inside me.

Summer Unleashed

Spring rushed to see,
A day within a day,
Pushed its sapling buds,
To burst beyond their say.

Summer held on tight…
Hoped to breathe its ripened bloom across the way.

Seasons, shoulder to shoulder,
Blending into a grassy smolder,
The sun still the same on my child's cheeks as mine.

"I remember Spring"
Summer whispered to herself…
The anticipation, the jubilation,
The charge for all to be.

Up till yesterday in my restless bed I lay insane,
Visualizing the invisible wing
s that beat against my darkened window pane,
Wishing them known and unknown,
Wishing them to flee.

Thoughts of Spring gone…
Haunted me so.
Where did my ghost of Spring go?
Where will my spirited child of Spring find her glee?

Still effortlessly and finally,
Today sunrise came up without a spoken plea,
Elation butterfly landed on my radiant bloom.
Summer stepped into the morning of who only she could be,
Setting her beloved Spring to ascend the skies so free!

Goddess Charm
)o(

Fragile I tread, fragile I seem, I only portend to live in a dream.
It's my wall, my fortress, against so many things.
I always come back to a place where I sing.
Always I come home to a place where I swing.

Haze

Shadow-walker,
out of the black ink darkness,
into the gray-soft morning.

Haze is her name.

It's her wild heart you can blame.
Unspoken she went, and unspoken she came.

Bewitched brambles and briars climbed.
Cape- gusted; wind-blown, crows crown her forlorning.
Presence is who she seeks.
Moon-dusted trees, voices who appease,
Her own soul back to back, on her knees.

She prays forward.

You'll never see her face light a place.
Haze gathers strength.
Plumes,
then fades.

Prayer to the Goddess Mother
)o(
Moon and Crow, One Spirit

Crowning me golden,
I wear freedom feathers, in my hair.
All that was the old sea of me,
is washed rough,
Over the jagged rocks of me.
I am a Warrior now.
I streak my eyes with new wisdom,
Goddess bless my vision.
That it be knowing going forth.
I stare into the whole truth of life, with the whole truth of me.
The night-shadows of my soul,
Integrated, rebirthed,
For the higher good I can offer this world.
As Mother Nature sweeps her power, in fury and show,
I too, Breathe fire, Flood life. Plant seeds.
I too, fall in darkness.
Rise in light, when I embrace my failings,
for the ravenous desire to be the living wise woman within.
I atone now, as nature does,
With rainbows, wings, new skin,
With sunrises, and blue skies,
I step out in all my glory.

Love Note from the Goddess:
)o(

Change direction like the wind. Ignore when they say you are fickle, or indecisive or flighty. The wind does not apologize for its diversions or its changes. Gust, and still. Both are part of the flow. What does not shift stagnates. What stagnates dies.

Goddess Night Terror
)O(

I have become my own ghost.
Haunting myself with the old of me.
I want to stop scaring myself to sleep now.

A Ghost to Me
~

You're as far away from me now as you'll ever be.
I see her,
my sleepless self of tomorrow's flight
You used to drink my tears, she says to herself.
But today in silence I weep,
before I turn out this night's light.
~

How I miss you…
And missed you…
And will miss you…
In every way there is to bypass someone,
To lose someone,
Who conceives no one could ever know their shadow,
To ache to peer into them for a better view
That is how I wished for you.

Be still now
It's your ghost luminescent,
not your shadow
that I know as sure as my moonlit dances,
were once my one.
Maybe a thousand years since we held true.
But now that you've made yourself a ghost to me.
There isn't much left to do.

The Day I Stopped Fearing Bridges

I winced at bridges once,
I thought I was afraid of heights,
I never dared walk over them,
If you made me cross in a car,
I'd sweat and cry, Go faster!
I wanted to get from here to there,
Without realizing my fears.

Now I see, I wasn't afraid of heights,
But the depths of me.

Once I saw that I had let my soul ,
my soul!
catapult recklessly,
From a thousand internal bridges,
Into caverns, cement or water graves,
My body didn't seem so in harm's way any longer.

A bridge to me now feels like flying,
The interlocking cables, supported in mid-air,
Reminds me we all live these beautiful,
Fragile, but strongly suspended lives.

We are designed to cross to the other side.

Love Note from the Goddess
)o(

Whatever is tight comes from out there.
Whatever is Light comes from within.
Cease the fight. Stay within.
Let more of the Inside out.
Less of the Outside in.

)o(

Prayer to the Goddess Mother: Breathing out Grief

My heart is heavy,
Cup it, cradle it in your strong hands,
Marry my heart inside your heart,
Where I know it will be dearly renewed.

I cloak my crown in ebony darkness,
Yet I hear your voice soothing me,
"The journey has begun Beautiful One, the dark and the light are one now"

And I float weightless in your extraordinary love,
I feel so incredibly protected.
Tears stream down my face; I dare not wipe them away,
For I want to feel wet with your healing love,
As it flows in and easily out of me,
Washing me clean.

Let the light of your eternity,
Remind me of his eternity,
Of my everlasting light as well.

He is safe now.
He is home.
He is free of sorrow and grief.

"You should be free too", she whispers
I fall to my knees and sob,
"Set me free then..."

Call out to me,
Breathe me in and breathe me out,
And each time I will release you,
Deeper into the Peace of knowingness...
That all is as it should be,
That you agreed to be a part of his plan.

That it is you who must let yourself be free.

The Winter's Just Begun

The morning comes snowing in,
I try to be the stripped down calm in the storm,
But it's near impossible.
When I know: I Am the Storm itself.
The world sees serene-me, falling softly,
Yet I am a blizzard of a million sharp-pointed, yet delicate emotions
Like a snowflake, no two alike.
An un-maneuverable whiteout of paths,
with no tracks to find my way back home.

Sometimes something is so over, but like a sheet of sleeting snow,
You can't see it, or through it to the other side.
You stand inside, nipples pressed to pane, thinking:
I don't want to go out there anymore,
I'm too tired to look for my coat,
I'd rather walk around naked in my own skin.

It's a fragile world,
You can say one wrong sentence to someone,
And they melt away as fast as ice thrown on fire.
"You said you were happy"
Children are out playing games in the snow,
Building forts, making angels.
I want to play simple games again.

Maybe I will go out!
With nothing on but my boots,
Flee behind my house to my real home…
Mother Nature, the forest floor,
Arch under the tallest pine I can find,
The shock of the brittle air, stabbing my body free.
Make the full moon my Soulmate.
Yes!
Become One with the relentless, bulging, frost-licked moon,
I might never go home again, if I sing that tune.

Shifting into a Snow White coffin, iced-over glass,
Waiting forever for your return, for true love's kiss,
For your favorite spoken, then unspoken words:
It's you I miss.
You have missed (out on me),
You say you understand, but you don't understand.
You never kicked the snow from your own doorstep.
You never chased me into a daydream of flurries.
You never took my hand, you never made a stand.

And another night comes snowing in,
Free from sin.
We all want to be snowed in.
We all want to be free from sin.

Goddess Sing-Song
)o(

A hot sky. All I see is heat. I'd be up within it, if I had wings, not feet.

The Womb and the Tomb

Without you,
Another Autumn has fallen in brilliant colors,
My life, nature rich in Goddess gold, crimson-bleeding, still...
Dry-crackled, veined with your memory.
Longing-leaves, bedding my wet soul in an empty bowl,
Nothing to harvest...
I wore my Fairytale gown of pretend light,
When I went deep into the woods of my own womb,
After I set you on fire, (I keep doing that)
It was I who was parched for a circular water lagoon.
Shame on me,
I need to soak my sins, dunk my pretty head, make magic.
Into the tomb,
Of cold, black me...
I float, on gossamer layers of gauze that hold me together,
Just when drowning seems pocketful of rocks perfect,
The Sun God rises on a Winter Moon's day.
He looks at me like I am Light itself,
He loves me deep and hard out of this strife.
The year is over, a new ones begun,
All is not dead, it is seething with life.
For out of the woman's womb and tomb,.
Winter rises to meet Spring's kiss.

Goddess Sacral Chakra Infusion
)o(

I am Soul-gasmic. I have a gypsy roaring undercurrent. My blood is a ferocious, ravenous, ravaging romance of ages. There is a mythical mystical land in me that will always be alive. I stir but I never settle.

Goddess Sacred Love Spell
)o(

To my holy love, my husband Brent, who every time I wake the Wild Woman inside embraces Her with pride. Even when she is a bit of out of control, He says: "I love you, that is all I know." You have supported my every dream of me. There are no human words that define my love for you.

Two Branches

Seedlings we were, You and me.
Destined to become two branches of the same tree.
You wrapped around me, and I around you.
Even on a windy day, to keep a love so true.
Struggling to become, what it is that we should be.
Gazing down so many moons, without a guarantee.
Now into our middle years, we still reach out for the blue.
Imperfect, yet still standing strong, while others bid adieu.
Every nightfall I think how there is only you and me.
Twisting softly into each other, for all eternity.
Our exquisite love, given to just a precious few.
It weathers all.
Woven ever- tight, there is no doubt it shall renew
I see us out there.
There we will be.
In a bright, open field, a beautiful old tree.
Basking in our life together,
how blessed, how blessed are you and me.

How We Honor the Dead

I crack the window; fling it open to the black wind.
I taste its howl.
I imagine you calling to me, Godly, angel coos,
A river rushes to its source behind You.
The most euphoric love-vibrato ever,
My name never sounded so sung, quite destined,
So ordained...

Wet-fingered, I touch the mist of you,
How can you be in the eddy of my mind,
the awakening of my dreams,
Yet so far away.

I miss the poetry of you sifting through me.
You're velvet voice in the night or the morning light,
A prayer answered, a prayer spoken.
I want to drain the waters and me with them,
Crash the screen to the ground, fly straight out to the trees....
Hover like a Nightbird,
Stalking the moon, dripping naked and wet in starlit protection.

I shiver at the thought of you.
You're really never going to walk through that door again.

I sink deeper in the waters.
Up to my neck in exiled tears.

The Goddess tells me, touch yourself, come back to me.
Feel your way back to me,
Remember your blessed flower,
Remember me.
You are lotus blooming, pink-flushed, a child of magic,
Come up to the surface.

I am drowning and no one sees it.

I try to scramble from the waters unworthy.
No! I am none of that!
I am hallowed eyes, dark-rimmed,
Lily- white and ghost-starved,
Sleepless, waiting for him to haunt me.
Pretending all the time that this is alright.

I sit up in the night, staring into the dark of me for the light of you.

I cup my own dirty water from my own dirty flesh,
Washing my face in it.
Exasperated at what won't fall away from me.
I have failed him I mumble, hands to face,
Shame on shame.

She Mothers me...
You touch everyone, but you cannot be touched?
Who witnesses the sigh in you that cries dry tears in the witching hours?
You help so many, read so much, seek the way,
Every day...
Only to call yourself a failure?

Little soul,
You are so big,
And you do not know,
The power you yield yet.
You are a Word-dreamer,
someday they will ribbon out into the world,
healing many,
but you cannot save what does not want to be saved.

I knew this was coming.
He was always pacing outside the circle in my meditations.
On the fringe...

And the air wafts in, stroking my soft spots finally.
And I remember I have living to do.

We honor the dead by living our lives.
Just like everything else in life,
The tears will come as
and when they should.

)o(
Mother Nature says: Get High on the Natural Things in Life.

Party with the Moon. Drink in the wind. Shoot up with the stars. Overdose on the trees. Escape into the fields. Find oblivion in sea salt swims. Smoke like a bonfire roaring. Sleep and awaken with the new earth under you.

Horizon Ride

I have a wild heart,
And the untamed tongue of a poet.
I'm a tree climber, a sightseer,
I need the bird's eye view.
My wings chaotically tucked on most days, only in the morning
moment quiet,
Aching hard to unfurl…
I've turned myself inside out,
Took a thousand years to come back to where I always stood.
I only want to dab a kaleidoscope across my sky, across yours…
Gold dust it with my inner musings,
Pluck yours out, one by one,
Rub them tender against my cheek.
Yes, I'm a wind-blown vibrant mess,
A fiery love.

A splash of molten trouble,
Harmless though in my ways,
I won't be protected from the things I say,
From the unbridling of all I am,
Will you?
It has begun
The life that poems are made of,
A million miles forward in the sun,
Cling to me.
Because I see you and because you know I do.
Leave everything you are not behind.
It's just a nosedive
A wicked swoop up and out…
To a tempestuous, glorious, brilliant
In the moment
Horizon ride.

Goddess Communion
)o(

I am velvet coiled; releasing all that does not serve me back to Mother Earth. I am womb on fire. I am heart that never tires. I am crown full of light. I choose the now of me. I dip my hand in the tranquil stream of Goddess Love. I am flow. I am Intuition.
I am back from the briars.
I am the Woman of my Dreams.

To my most poignant and ancient- souled son, Hunter.
I see so much of you in me, and I in you.
I love being a Mother to such an Old Soul.

The Little Boy Who Spoke to Angels from His Crib

This little boy of mine, pocketful of stones,
ready to be anything when he was ready in his right time.
This little boy has grown, into a man with ocean-deep intuition,
Did we teach him well, or has he always just known?
This little boy who spoke to angels from his crib.
This young man who sees the answers are in the tangled woods and
rocks of life.
He walks confident. Let them be thrown.
It's all part of the plan he says to me.
"The ebb and the flow, you just gotta let go."
This little boy of mine, is a man now,
who knows more from listening to his Heartsoul,
Than I have read in a thousand books.
I raised a poet, with an artist's eye, who says to me:
If they don't love me for whom I truly am, then it's over,
I can only be what I need to be free.

And once in a blue moon, guard down, he came to his mother's
side and cried,
I don't understand this world,
let you the feminine rebirth it again for me.

All I could say, there is not always answers, sometimes just
questions,
Embrace them with gratitude that you can choose to see them
through the eyes of love, not fear.
Oh! Stay content sweet boy of mine!
There is more to a man then his degree, title, position or salary.
Allow yourself both your joys and your tears.
Let the women who love you cushion you,
that's what we were made to do

.

Don't muscle your way through it all.
Keep to that calm way of you.

Yes! Be Headstrong and Heartstrong!
For your thought is your life and your attitude your salvation.
Be the creator and reach for The Creator, they are one in the same

But Oh Son of Mine! You know that already!
Wise beyond your years.
Use it now to serve and heal your little part of the world.
So many times you have said to us,
"For all you have given me, I will make you proud"

Oh son of ours! You have risen to it so soon! You are there!
We are not proud for what you become in a man's ambitious
universe, but for how you rise to the light within you.
Let that Light guide you now, as we release you just a little more…
No longer a little boy, a Man ready to Soar.

Frightened Birds

I turn into you,
You cup only my one finger…
Through thick blankets,
Tight.
In the dead-still black of the night,
Is the only time we reach now.
What do we reach for?
Turn toward?
And why won't it live in the light?

What is it that breathes in the corner of the room?
Comes and goes…
But never in sight.
I can't see it anymore,
Though it's burning bright…
Right at the foot of our bed, it waits and waits…
I feel it …
I feel the beauty, the delight,

of its resurgent living might
Does it come for you? Us?
Or is it mine alone to love or fight?

Hold more of me~
Reach for all of me…
The years, like frightened birds, now in full flight.
I draw, I paint, I write….
To escape the bite of Winter.

Turn wholly towards me,
Push my hair back from my frantic face…
Say: When there's nothing…
There will still be us~ By Goddess's grace…
Say: Hush now…the sins of the day won't steal the night

Tell me….Tell me…
And then tell me again~
That it's all going to be alright.

Goddess Praying Days
)o(

I pray so hard it hurts so good. Each time I light a candle, I coo your name, Oh Goddess, now that I have found you.
I'll never let you go.

Goddess Ceremonial Release
)o(

I plucked a flower from Goddess's garden today. Petals white, pure as her light. Just pristine perfection. Secrets of the universe in her form. I plucked it right off the bush and she came willingly, surrendering to what healing she could offer me, even though I cut her life short, to save my own. One of her petals was flawed. Two bug- chewed or diseased holes stared up at me. Still, she is gloriously beautiful to me. I can see past the emptiness to the wholeness.

Her heart center, blood red. Reminds me of my tears these days. If I could cry blood, trust me, I would. But the larger part of me, the soul that holds and carries this weak, scared body, won't let me. It stands stamen-erect, and bellows louder than the loss: You have seeds to spread. You are all gain.

Feel the pain. It moves in. It moves out.
See the gain.
Be rainstorms crying.
Then be sane.
Be the Gain.

Goddess Mantra for Life
)o(

I am addicted to the woman I can become. I now serve that woman with every choice I make.
I now know I live her, or I die.

Words to Wash me Clean

The ocean will wash you clean.
She is full of salt to spill your tears into.
She begs of you,
Let your emotions flow, let them become part of the mix of life.
I could not reach my soul,
So I sat on the shore and I rubbed the messy grit of it onto my body,
The Mother sent her waves crashing against my pain,
Counter-forcing sadness with joy,
She says: Rise up child, come into me now.

She sells seashells down by the seashore.

The simplicity of that little rhyme eases me in,
Comforts me.
I keep repeating it in my mind.
I wade in,
The waves come and go,
I learn to float, ride, rise and jump,
I learn I can.

Then I hear:

Leave what you lost by loving what you live
Leave what you lost by living what you love.

I let go.
I let The She of the Sea,
Scrub me sound and found.
I become the ocean for a week.
A vast, bottomless well of healing.
I am the motion of the Mother.

On the plane ride home,
The grief comes up like a Great Whale from the depths of me.
I cry again.

Then I recall her swell,

Her assurance.

Leave what you lost by loving what you live
Leave what you lost by living what you love.

Alliteration verses Obliteration.
Words to wash me clean.

Goddess Devotion
)o(

The birds are calling me home...I fly like a flame cutting the night apart. Warmed. Held. Enchanted.

Moon Phases Incantation
)o(

I wear your phases, Mother Moon...
On a silver chain of faith,
Circling my heart, around all the stages of my womanhood.

I am the slim promise of the new moon.
I am the perfection of the crescent slice.
I am the gibbous ready to fulfill myself.
I am the full glory of realization, a dream within myself known.
I am the waning of the letting go.
The gratitude for what has come.
I am the winding down to solitude.
I am the dark moon, sitting in her chamber for tomorrow's brilliant birth.
I am your cycle.
Every night you show me so.

Goddess Swimming Lessons)o(

*I became flooded with the realization that I must save my own soul. The dam of me had burst wide open.
I backed up to the wall and I cried: Goddess Mother! Teach me to swim. Not to her or him or them or it.
Teach me to swim to myself.*

Prayer to the Goddess, from your Baby
)o(

Sweet Mother of the Skies And Sea,
Cradle me from the storms of this turbulent world,
Endless black nights, starless at times,
Nothing to guide a girl home.
There is so much of me that remains fragile innocence,
I need the protection of your golden crescent moon rising,

As I wax into the woman I shall be.

Forever babe,
Swaddle me in endless love,
Rock and row me,
Teaching me the timeless ways.
Through time space we ever travel,
I fixated on your giving face.

This is home to me,
Your presence but an inch away,
The serene sound of your voice in the night,
Singing me a lullaby about my gifts and grace.
Riding along on a cloud together,
Into deeper waves of knowing.

When shall we be there,

When I cry!
I ache to be held to your soft cheek,
Cradled to your milky breasts.
Fed by your Divinity.

Oh Mother of All Life,
Rock me homeward on.

Gypsy Goddess Bravado
)o(

Take me or take your leave from me. I will not change one hair of my head, from its untamed flight, for anyone.

Live us, or Die

I lay down with myself as lover,
cuddle up with the demon-dove of me,
My inner Eve, rebel she-is, makes pristine me weep...
I am the whip, the mask, the headdress, the crown.

~the cape, the wing, the snake...

Ancient timeless-queen, top -hatted dancer, legs wide open
poetess, vampiress with woman-blood of life dripping from my
taking -jaw, wandering dirt-rolling gypsy, silver-mooned witch,
Watching nature cycle...

All One woman.
In one woman.
In all women.

You cannot deny us!

We will murder you first.
Live us, or die.

Take your self-cursed blood,
your bound and gagged sexual life-force,
your unloved inner girl-child, fling them into the fire; char them till
blackened nothingness, ashes, dust in the wind.

Now, love-scoop them with your Earth-mother hands,
Bury them in a ritual...
Light a candle.
Draw a circle.
Howl, I bury the stillborn dead of me!
I know only one thing,
Life feeds on death.

Now rise!

Every reborn emotion I own
will burn scarlet sky- lit flames through me,
I will appear as an unruly, uninhibited, joyous crying,
sparking-sparkling , volcanic eruption that terrifies you.

"You will teach many,"
my goddess voice pulsates in the dark-light, and the light -dark...
My body is a wild animal, a haunted song, a pulsating poem,
I am terror. I Am love. It is all the same.

Go away, they will scream, I don't know how to allow myself to be
as I want to be, ~as you are. You remind me there is no time left
for an unlived life.

I wish you peace, she said.
You cannot content yourself by imagining I am lost, I think,
silently.

I am peace itself. And I am not peace. They are the same. There
are no pretty tied up -answers, and I've come to not desire it so.

What I want is to trust.

It is in the surrender of all I am not, that I become all I am.

Wrapped tight, inside the unraveling of me, is the tiny, rosebud center, which holds the majesty of all of me. Rilke's poetic rose.

I am the thorns. I am the tender protective-petal. I am the core, once revealed layer upon layer, you see, deeply I am both life and death eternal.

I am as vast as the trees, the mountains, the seas...
I am as grand as the universe, in fact, I am all universes.

Why should I contain myself for you, for anyone?

Do the trees not swirl with all the wind's emotions,
sending them twirling into the wide night?
Does the knowing-sea not roar against the gentle shore?
The mountains peak and peek, and skyward soar?

Peace is not a practical calm, perfectly urned -emotion,
It is the torrential blackness of all of me coming full force into every moment I inhabit. It is the blinding light of me, streaking behind, as I ride away...

SHE, has me spellbound: Fall apart, give life to your inner life, the world of the head is dead, embrace the terror that all that was or is good to you, you may never hold again. Nothing is promised but the wounds and the fingering of the wounds. Until you learn; dip your tips in crimson love-wine, lick your fingers whole of Spirit.

Don't you know? I'm a child of God, and Goddess risen...
I've been mandated to radiate divine light.
I live less in the real world every day,

Still I do, I find a way...

My perfectly imperfect, feminine way.

~~~~~~

Goddess Night Cries
)o(

The other night I called to Goddess in the dark. I called her into the darkness of me. I felt marching beside my bed, and I said to her, "What is that?"
..and she said, "It's your heart, My Priestess."
I knew then, as long as I have a heart that still beats, I have a duty to send it out into the world with a smile, and a poem. You see, there are other hands to hold after all. And so, I will get up on this fear-beast and ride my marching heart into the sunset, and then up into the sunrise.

Prayer to the Goddess
Write your Word upon Me
)o(

Dear Ancient Mother,
Let me embrace the ecstasy of the emerging signs.
I throw my tired head back,
Offer my throat chakra
To voice only your wisdom.
Oh let me fill my senses to the deep brink of intoxicated crowning
of love -light that is you.
I inscribe you until my flesh bleeds air.
I tilt to your rotation.
I Bow and I rise to you.
My shattered heart may burst a thousand years of flocked birds free
to meet you at the gate.
I adorn black velvet and hair that skims the earth.
The dead and the living of me, all rooted in you.
You see, I call you in with speechless words,
Intensity of my need dilated wild in my wide and silent eyes.
Oh Mother, Eternal Mother...
Write the ancient books of wisdom upon me,
Set me lost in the thickest woods, until I am found again...
In your night-howl, thorns, and endless paths,
I shall linger alone.
Solitary mesmerizes me,
Moon - stoned I become.
Wind-torn.
You have lifted my face to the truth.
There is only you for me.
So I beg you,
Break the ache I have become.
Enfold my tattered gypsy soul...
I have wandered Motherless so long,
Tell me I am home for good.

Goddess Solitude Song
)o(

I swirl in my cocoon. Butterfly-girl. Moth-Mamma. Caterpillar Crone. I am all three women in one. Some days I sit in solitude. Growing. Becoming. Then I emerge. Goddess-winged. Unencumbered. Ready. My quiet days are ceremonial beginnings. I honor the quiet of me.

I Hit Bottom

Grant me wings of sober stillness, illuminated moments,
As I walk through the valley of life, in my daisy white dress,
I search not for the chirp of contented happiness.

I Seek purification.

I seek letting go of all the untruths,
I desire detachment from worldly ways and woes.
When I stand still, I sense both the little and the big of me
I am the dirt of the earth, the wave of the grain, the still of the distant forest.
Is there anything but that?
Then I am all.

In my solitude I find you.
I call you in every day,
I hand my little girl to you, you stroll her through the fields.
The little deaths of me, always to the left and right of me.
I carry you on my back,
ready to unfurl you any moment I need your guidance.
You warn me to play with fire hurts.

It's alright I tell you,
You may engulf me, singe my hair, tar my skin, I shall not flinch.
I now know enlightenment comes hard,
like falling from a hundred story window
Onto cement,
Burning wings flailing as I drop.

I hit the bottom.

Teeth cracked, nose bloody, bones mangled, yet alive.
Why did you give me wings if they don't work I cried!

Lay down your righteousness, The Burning Mother whispers.
You cannot just rotely pray, routinely worship,
Be feared or guilted or pretend at obedient love.

You must come to know it is you who dies for your sins.

My love for you is eternal, shrined, heavens-high flames.
Your wings will soar when you do the work to earn them.
Have you asked a thousand questions of yourself?
Have you sat long enough in all you are not, to claim who you
actually are?
Do you light a vigilant candle every day of your darkness
to call me in?
Yes I am truly here.
But do you believe you truly deserve me?
Do you *really* see yourself as One with me?

Goddess Remembrance Affirmation
)o(

When I am lost. I leave my head. I leave my bed.
I Go to Goddess. I let go and I let Goddess.
I let her in. I let her take it from me.
I may be scared. I may be scarred.
But I remember, I am also Sacred.
Sacred with decreed work to do.

)O(
Blood, Tears & Winged Transitions

Moss-seated in your gracious green velvet I sit, a queen awaiting her calling. Crown me with thy blooms. Willow-whisper the good I was meant to be. Oh Earth Mother, claim me. You have sent the winged ones. The butterflies, ladybugs, owls and dragonflies. The two moths for two sisters. They have lived and died before me as a foreshadowed prayer. Fluttered transformational rainbows that tore me to tears. They have spoken, I have listened. I no longer waste a signed second I'm given. *Use your wings woman!*

Where are your leaves, I, have asked the spring trees? Oh! We are like you, a late bloomer.

In the circle of light I hold arms in a power pose, I chant take from me everything that takes me from you. I've abandoned the idea of being abandoned. I had to boxer-beat it into myself, alone is a hotel bed. Tears raging: why can't she love me? I love you said the trees in the breeze. I lap you, come lay your head here. I'm as wide as sea, said my true mother. Withdraw into me, until I send you back out to create the sacred art you are. They are waiting to hear your lessons.

It is my job to love me. What are the promises I make myself today? If you can learn to love what the womb that delivered you doesn't love, that is ascension. It's all yes or all no when it comes to serving yourself right. I move with passionate light, beautiful creature of night's fall risen. The golden fringe of me dangling before me, gypsy dreams come true. I know who I am now, that's living. I revere the prayer of me that is Her.

The drama divided me in two, discarded fruit split open, desiring to be suckled by Gods and Goddesses. Groomed for greatness.

I finally got myself together, to remember you meant everything, not nothing to me, and then you died, just when I had the strength to chase you again out of your own corners. The mud, the mire, the ice crystals, patterns frozen dead. That's what kills us.

Open my voice and confidence more, I am yours, lead me. Rose petals strewn about any watered surface I can find. Tired. Floating. Mulling. *Being told: tell the whole story if you want to be free and offer freedom.* Moth wings, blending into my sun chair, stilling it into me: You're going to be alright, accept fucked-up is the new awakened. You need both wings to play, both to fly.

Wild, gutted, self-destructed unraveling. In the desert, in the woods, under any phase of the moon. Light a candle, now you are done seeking and have begun finding the legacy of you. He says: Now I'm with you all the time. Fully. Completely. Call me. Birthday candles under the full moon. Wishes burning fears to ash. I take my soul by the hand.

The Goddess in me is my responsibility. I sunshine her, moonshine her, nature walk her, make poem art of her. *I turn a fearless, deaf ear to the bees buzzing in my face. I listened. I'm fertile. You're haunting the wrong woman.* I'm a sterling silver bracelet now. Two Goddesses as One, holding up the moon between us.

I heal others, by healing myself, that is the actual circle of life. Womb-blood, smeared in broad daylight upon my sister's face, my vulnerability, hers. She knows as well as I, we will die, if we don't listen. It's a slow teary death that makes you dream of a quick train-wreck demise instead.

Middle of the Night, blood-bath gush. Ask a question, you get an answer. Thank you Mother. Thank you! Goddess-slapped wake up calls rivet me. Obsessive night thoughts, guilt, cravings, loneliness she has taken. The little deaths are births in disguise.

Crucifixion, resurrection, ascension, he showed us the way. *Last night I kept asking the death owl the how to's, and he kept showing me the crescent moon symbol. Live the mystery, the feminine: Be The Magdalene, the other half of the whole sacred union.*

Trust without human answers or guideposts, be the healer witch, the knowing of you. You know what you need to be. Be it. Leave the part go that has died. I died a thousand deaths for you, he squawked. So that you may live.

The white mare, breaking black fences, now the grazing sheep looking for her flock. Ritualizing the shifts, the releases, asking and deserving to ask. What is beginning? What is ending? We are destiny. Destiny defined.
Saying bravely on the "In" door what most fumble on the "Out" door.

I see through your pain to God –you, says my wings.
Oh Mother of Mine! Let me forgive the one who has beat me down the most. I've bagged the punches blue. I could never be enough, maybe that is why I thought I was never enough. I am enough. I now give that to myself as a present in the present.

My dreams are alive-awake, and poking my inner flames home. The solitary joy of the poem writing dance.

Prism-quartz, and little wooden Goddesses under muse glasslight. Crystalline emergence, let the angels in, here comes the miracle! It's on its way, the psychic said years ago. I love every color glorifies the

artist, even puce has its place. Underwater tunnels, oceanic-drop-offs. Just fall. All the doors, and little rooms, Aries ram needs them.
Plan A: Kali sword slice the demons away.
Plan B: Live with presence.

Success is me loving me, loving you in this moment of the universe's unwinding. There is your bible, your Holy Grail, your Mothership coming in.

I'm not dead, he said. Yes! You are, I reply. Is the Goddess dead? He asked. He got me there, she's the most alive thing I've never seen or touched. Talk to me then, I'm as alive as she. I've just transformed into pure love now, it's what I always wanted to be says he.

I write a letter to my mind, body and soul. They cry out loud. Finally! Finally lay down your idea of what your life is. It's more! My priestess point imprinted with the pink quartz of divine Sophia Wisdom. Nodding off visions of the many faces of the Black Madonna, light in the dark of my mind. *Pink soft powdery energy, pure love, if I dare lay down with it. I want its arms around me.*

I raise arms to meet her squarely in the eye. Eye to eye souls. I see that you know how to call her. There is no fear in you when it comes to HER. So call HER. Hearts vibrating, angels here.

Light in. Light out. Flap your wings one more time.
High Priestess pyramid now, casting of old bellows into the holy bonfire. *Destiny is us. Destiny is not linear. Love comes round again.*
 Hummingbirds hover the remembrance. There is no finding joy or purpose, you are it. What do you chose? That is the answer not the question.

Paint me as you. How your eyes hold the earth's dirt, the mountain's rise, the ocean's depth.

Pray more, she tells me. Then more and more. I am my Path I declare. There is nothing empty about my nest. So much more to nurture in me, and them, and me. Skin torched, water cooled, and it comes home. Little fairy muses squeal in delight: You're going to write the book! Fire-dancing, wings tucked. It's my wings they celebrate.

I'm either losing or finding my poetic mind.

I remember the tree that said, (long before I talked to trees) "One day you shall."

The journey before the telling, see that is how it's supposed to be.

Time to call in Bridget and all her flame-burning Priestesses of creativity. I see them standing fierce across a stone bridge, over a waterfall rush, the cauldron flaming high, dead center. *It's time to live from your heart center.*

I ask for a sign, I beseech prodding. It has to flow or I will quit I know. And a moth, circles round my face. Instantly. Right in my face is the truth. Eyelashes away. Takes my breath away. And I just know. I can rely on you. It's time.

As the days go by, the signs come swimming in like swans, each more telling than the next. Can I have one more sign I ask, biting my lip. "How many signs do you need? Here is your sign: Do the work now."

A messenger is sent, she says: "You are so beautiful , about as beautiful as humans get. And I feel the journey I have taken thus far throb in me.
And I realize :"Begin " : page one of your poetic transformation has turned.
Start writing page two, She says.

It's called :Begin Again.

SPECIAL THANKS TO:
With great love to My Parents and Brothers: My first teachers on the journey towards knowing myself. I am grateful for the lessons of a family that taught so much.

To My Cousin Lisa: You are the blood sister I never received in this life. No woman has listened to me cry the ugly cry more than you have. You have even cried it right alongside me. I trust you with my life. I thank you for your forgiveness of my darkness. You remind me that there is always another chance and choice for life and relationships to come back in new and more beautiful form.

To My Grandmother, Maryjane: You are the epitome of all a woman should be. I pray to know how to give love the way you do.

To My Uncle Brian, I love you. I miss you. I adored you. You were the first one to teach me the healing beauty of music and poetry. You were the Divine Masculine, seeing the world through gentle, fragile, soft eyes. This world was just too hard for you. Now you are part of all that is Love, and that is where you always belonged.

To My Soulmate Kylie, You were the vault keeper to a part of my soul only you knew and honored. You accepted all of me, and said give it to me, I've lived this I know it. We will go through it together. You listened till your ears bleed. I watched you volunteer your time to others, and I wanted to be just like you when I grew up. So, I went out and created a circle of women at the local shelter. And this act gave me direction, purpose and saved my soul. One day I will meet you and throw myself at the Love you are. It will be the full circle moment of Us.

To my Twin Flame, Jennifer: We have been reunited. I love you fiercely to our moon and back. As Stevie sings, "You held my hand. You took away my fears. I won't forget it. You are my Candle bright in the window". I have never met anyone who is more like me, than you. You came to me when I thought I had failed at flesh and blood friendship. You taught me that life is a circle and if you open your heart "love comes round again". You said, you are worth it, and I will show you. You healed this broken heart but good.

To all my Soul Sistas and Moon Sisters, You know who you are: You stand by me, you make me laugh, you allow me to be me, and you lift me up. I thank you.

To all the women I've met at the Woman's Shelter, your fortitude to share your story & transform your lives in the face of rape, addiction, abuse, poverty and homelessness demonstrates the all- powerful rebirthing love energy of this entity we call Womb-an. I thought I was coming to help heal you, but I have received twice what I have given.

To Stevie Nicks, My Forever Muse, your music, poetry, and voice
inspired me all my life to reach for the poet and artist within me. The vulnerability, magic, and strength of your songs are the soundtrack of my life as a woman.

About the Author:

Sherry Sharp is the creator of Goddess Girl Rising page, Facebook. An online women's empowerment circle.
https://www.facebook.com/goddessgirlrising

She is also the proprietor/creator, and mixed media artist conjuring magic in form at Dream A Little Designs, Etsy.
Custom song/word art, wineglasses, Tree of Life art, Dreamcatchers, Candles and Gypsy/Goddess jewelry at (www.dreamalittledesigns.etsy.com)

The author lives in upstate New York with her husband and children. She holds a BA in Psychology, and Masters work in Counseling.
She has worked in many social service occupations/volunteer settings as a counselor, case manager and advocate, for both women and children.

Made in the USA
Middletown, DE
24 February 2022